From the Ganges to the Hudson

THE NEW IMMIGRANTS SERIES

Allyn & Bacon

Series Editor, Nancy Foner, State University of New York at Purchase

Changing Identities: Vietnamese Americans, 1975-1995, by James M. Freeman

From the Workers' State to the Golden State: Jews from the Former Soviet Union in California, by Steven J. Gold

From the Ganges to the Hudson: Indian Immigrants in New York City, by Johanna Lessinger

Salvadorans in Suburbia: Symbiosis and Conflict, by Sarah J. Mahler

A Visa for A Dream: Dominicans in the United States, by Patricia R. Pessar

From the Ganges to the Hudson:
Indian Immigrants in New York City

Johanna Lessinger

Allyn and Bacon

Boston • London • Toronto • Sydney • Tokyo • Singapore

Contents

Foreword to the Series

The United States is now experiencing the largest wave of immigration in the country's history. The 1990s, it is predicted, will see more new immigrants enter the United States than in any decade in American history. New immigrants from Asia, Latin America, and the Caribbean are changing the American ethnic landscape.

Until recently, immigration was associated in the minds of many Americans with the massive influx of southern and eastern Europeans at the turn of the century. Since the late 1960s, America has again become a country of large-scale immigration, this time attracting newcomers from developing societies of the world. The number of foreign-born is at an all-time high: nearly 20 million foreign-born persons were counted in the 1990 census. Although immigrants are a smaller share of the nation's population than they were earlier in the century—8 percent in 1990 compared to about 15 percent in 1910—recent immigrants are having an especially dramatic impact because their geographic concentration is greater today. About half of all immigrants entering the United States during the 1980s moved to eight urban areas: Los Angeles, New York, Miami, Anaheim, Chicago, Washington, D.C., Houston, and San Francisco. America's major urban centers are, increasingly, immigrant cities with new ethnic mixes.

Who are the new immigrants? What are their lives like here? How are they redefining themselves and their cultures? And how are they contributing to a new and changing America? The *New Immigrants Series* provides a set of case studies that explores these themes among a variety of groups. Each book in the series is written by a recognized expert who has done extensive in-depth ethnographic research on one of the immigrant groups. The groups represent a broad range of today's arrivals, coming from a variety of countries and cultures. The studies cover a wide geographical range as well, based on research done in different parts of the country, from New York to California.

Most of the books in the series are written by anthropologists. All draw on qualitative research that shows what it means to be an immigrant in America today. As part of each study, individual immigrants tell their stories, which will help give a sense of the experiences and problems of the newcomers. Through the case studies, a dynamic picture emerges of the way immigrants are carving out new lives for themselves at the same time as they are creating a new and more diverse America.

The ethnographic case study, long the anthropologist's trademark, provides a depth often lacking in research on immigrants in the United States. Many anthropologists, moreover, like a number of authors in the *New Immigrants Series,* have done research in the sending society as well as in the United States. Having field experience at both ends of the migration chain makes anthropologists particularly sensitive to the role of transnational ties that link immigrants to their home societies. With first-hand experience of immigrants in their home culture, anthropologists are also well positioned to appreciate continuities as well as changes in the immigrant setting.

As the United States faces a growing backlash against immigration, and many Americans express ambivalence and sometimes hostility toward the latest arrivals, it becomes more important than ever to learn about the new immigrants and to hear their voices. The case studies in the *New Immigrants Series* will help readers understand the cultures and lives of the newest Americans and bring out the complex ways the newcomers are coming to terms with and creatively adapting to life in a new land.

NANCY FONER
Series Editor

Acknowledgments

Whatever the mythology, intellectual work cannot be carried out alone. I owe thanks to a great many people and institutions for their help and encouragement over the years. A Rockefeller Foundation grant in immigration made the first stages of this research possible. During that period His Excellency the late Arun Patwardhan and Mr. Talmiz Ahmad of the Indian Consulate in New York opened many doors for me and also paid me the complement of sincere interest in what I was doing. The late Vera Rubin and the staff of the Research Institute for the Study of Man offered crucial administrative services which made it possible for an unaffiliated scholar to receive a Rockefeller grant.

Members of a long-running anthropology study group, Eva Friedlander, Betty Levin, Frances Rothstein, Nina Glick Schiller, Ida Susser, Linda Basch and Sam Beck, have given me sustained intellectual support for years as well as acting as a cheering section when I grew discouraged. I am particularly indebted to Nina Schiller for her insights into ethnicity and transnationalism.

Smita Biswas, Nilanjana Chatterjee, Shekar Ramakrishnan, Frances Rothstein and Rita Sethi read and commented helpfully on drafts of portions of this book. Leslie Lessinger has with great affection supported my work, both literally and metaphorically, for more than 30 years. Estelle Strizhack has shared her knowledge of immigration procedure and an abiding love of India. Bonnie Nuzum and the staff of the Writers' Space in Brooklyn provided the serene physical setting where this book could be written. Editors Nancy Foner and Sylvia Shepard have been encouraging, patient and thorough. Finally I owe a tremendous debt of gratitude to the hundreds of Indian immigrants who have shared their thoughts and experiences with me. I only regret that they have to remain anonymous.

Introduction

In some sense the research for this ethnography about Indian immigrants in New York began long ago and very far away. I was a naive graduate student in anthropology in 1967, sent by my university to do three months of field work training on the Caribbean island of Trinidad. There, looking for a field site, I encountered for the first time what has since come to be called the Indian diaspora, the Indian communities created by migration around the world. The families I eventually lived with in Trinidad and most of the women traders I interviewed were descended from Indian immigrants who had come to Trinidad in the 19th and early 20th centuries. The grandchildren and great grandchildren of indentured Indian sugar workers I met were both identifiably Trinidadian and at the same time culturally distinct from their Afro-Trinidadian neighbors. There was a good deal of economic and political tension between the two groups, often expressed in ethnic/racial terms.

Returning to the U.S. after three months to write an M.A. thesis, I was forced to think about questions of migration, cultural retention and ethnicity. What did it mean to be a Caribbean of Indian ancestry? And what, if any, was the relationship of these people with the India their ancestors had left many generations earlier? At that time much of the social scientific discussion about Indo-Caribbeans focused on their retention of Indian cultural patterns in the face of time and distance. Thus it was easy to look on India itself as the fountainhead of "true" or "authentic" Indian culture. There was a slight suspicion that Indians of the diaspora, such as those in Trinidad, lived a diluted, watered-down version of Indian culture; a professor assured me that I should go to India to see "the real thing."

It was only later that I developed a more sophisticated and dialectical view of immigration, and came to understand that Indian immigrant culture, whether in Trinidad or the United States, is a vital, living force in its own right. Furthermore the development of modern India and the development of Indian immigration are today two parts of a single phenomenon which needs to be studied as a whole.

Not surprisingly, when it later came time for me to chose a site for Ph.D. work, I chose India. I spent almost two years doing research on markets and traders in the large South Indian city of Madras in 1971 and 1972. Since then I have returned often, pursuing further research in Madras and traveling in other parts of the country. I lived there most recently in 1991-92, investigating the entry of working-class women into employment in export garment factories. This 20-year experience in India has been of tremendous importance to the present work since I have actually watched India as it has been drawn more completely into a global economy and has simultaneously entered a new period of out-migration as extensive as that of the 19th century.

In the India of 1971 only a handful of middle-class people or entrepreneurs had been abroad to work or study. On returning to India they were considered daring and sophisticated and derived a good deal of prestige from their knowledge of life in other countries. Madras, the city I know best, remained deeply traditional, more resistant to foreign influences than many northern Indian cities. By 1991, however, major changes were visible. Madras had begun to be a cosmopolitan city. Although it lagged behind Bombay, Delhi, or such rivals as Bangalore, it was full of high tech and export industries and entrepreneurs who had arrived there from other parts of India to make money. Accompanying these changes was a vastly increased level of overseas migration. Virtually every middle-class family, and many working-class families as well, had relatives and friends who had lived abroad for extended periods or who had left India for good. These migrants had sent home money, consumer items and new ideas, hastening the reshaping of local culture.

The result of this greater social and economic contact with the West and the greater social integration of different regions of India is that many younger Indians now plan early in life to migrate. Already a great many families' kinship and friendship networks are spread out around the globe. The point has been brought home to me directly as I and my family have been drawn into these transnational relationships. Once, when I departed India I vanished as a social person for my Indian friends until I reappeared again. Today, as the New York node in Indian friends' extended kin networks, I and my family play host to Indian visitors, give advice about American college admission, scholarships and job prospects to fictive "nieces" and "nephews," and engage in the inevitable exchange of family photos and gifts which mark our enduring relationships.

It was logical, therefore, that in 1984 I began a study of Indian immigrants in New York, with the help of a Rockefeller Foundation grant on immigration. The first study focused on interviews with large numbers of businessmen, a handful of businesswomen, and a number of professionals who had formed, or planned to form, their own businesses. Since then the research has continued more broadly if less intensively. I have gone on attending Indian immigrant events, reading the immigrant press and discussing a wide variety of issues with the Indian immigrants I meet—students, waiters, intellectuals, shop clerks, professionals and religious specialists. For this book I also conducted a series of interviews with activists involved in various Indian or South Asian social and political issues. When I first began my research in 1984 the businesspeople and professionals dominated the discourse within the local Indian population. Today their often conservative view of the world is being contested by younger and more liberal or radical people.

Over the ten years I have been observing New York's Indian immigrants, the population has continued to grow through new migration, and its centers of concentration continue to disperse to the suburbs of New York's greater metropolitan area. The greater New York area still offers the jobs, housing, and social ambience Indian immigrants want. During this same period, India itself has become more acutely aware of Indian migrants and has made increasing efforts to connect with and claim overseas Indian populations in the U.S., Canada, Europe and Australia. Perhaps the greatest change in New York is that a younger generation, often born or raised in the U.S., is reaching adulthood and beginning to make its opinions felt, and is doing so at a period of increasing racial antagonism and anti-immigrant feeling in the larger U.S. society.

Inevitably, in a short ethnography like this I end up omitting some things, oversimplifying others and making a number of generalizations. At the same time, I have tried to give some sense of the multiple voices and contending points of view which exist within this population. Indians are not a single monolithic unit. Like every ethnic group, this one is internally divided, full of contestation and debate, and changing rapidly. In particular I am concerned to show the class stratification among Indian immigrants, since this has been underplayed in previous accounts, and to discuss the newer activist organizations as they bid for recognition as part of "the community."

This book contains many quotations and a number of case studies in an effort to give a human face to an immigration process which is, in my view, filled with ambivalence and emotional pain as well as achievement and success. In using people's words or details of their lives to illustrate my points, every effort has been made to conceal individual identities. In the case studies, people's names, cities of origin and other details have been altered or obscured to prevent recognition and embarrassment. Although the people I interviewed spoke to me freely, sometimes brutally frankly, and knew I was a researcher, most would dislike having details of their lives exposed to public gaze. I am confident that none of my informants can be identified in these case studies. In a more general way, however, I hope than Indian immigrants will recognize themselves, and feel that aspects of their lives have been truthfully described.

The organization of this book moves from the general to the particular. Chapter 1 places Indian immigration to the New York metropolitan area in national and historical perspective. It also introduces one of the book's main themes: the creation of Indian ethnic identity in the context of evolving American concepts of race and ethnicity. Like other "new immigrants," Indians confront a rising tide of racism and anti-immigrant sentiment in the U.S. along with counter-movements towards pluralism and inclusion.

Chapters 2 and 3 introduce the ethnic infrastructure, the patterns of consumption, and the institutions and networks by which New York area Indians define their identity and live their daily lives. These two chapters also make clear that Indian immigrants are highly transnational, remaining intimately connected with people and events in India. The fashions, political debates, cultural developments and religious movements of India spill over into Indian immigrant life here, intensified by the fact that many immigrants regularly move back and forth between India and the U.S. At the same time immigrants have an influence on Indian society and Indian political developments. Chapter 4 returns to these questions of transnationalism and a global economy, asking why, and under what conditions, people choose to migrate to the U.S. That chapter looks at the emergence of a transnational or diasporic Indian identity in more detail.

Chapter 5 looks at family and gender relationships, and the emerging voices of the second generation. Almost universally, the children of immigrants experience special problems and unique kinds of emotional stress arising from their "in between" status. Indian immigrant children are no exception. Raised and partly socialized in the U.S., and thus in some ways more American than their parents, they are nevertheless separated from their non-immigrant peers by the racial identity U.S. society assigns them as well as by culture, by a sense of ethnic identity—and by their intense emotional involvement with and loyalty to their families.

Chapter 6 looks at a rising tide of social activism among Indian immigrants which addresses the kinds of problems—from wife beating to racial discrimination—that a more traditional Indian immigrant leadership has tended to ignore. For the younger generation, questions of gender, race and ethnic identity take on new meanings and have to be renegotiated. The chapter asks how this activism challenges and redefines what it means to be Indian-American or an American of South Asian descent in the New York of the 1990s.

Theoretically, the book's approach relies on concepts of political economy. My account emphasizes employment and economic forces, and the resulting formation of class divisions, in defining Indian immigrant culture. At the same time, I take advantage of newer approaches to immigration which emphasize the complex, fluid, multi-layered and contextual nature of immigrant cultural identities (see for instance Roosens 1989). As what Espiritu and others call a "visible minority" (Espiritu 1992:6), Indian immigrants in the U.S. do not have absolute freedom to define themselves. Nevertheless the debates which continue to rage within the Indian immigrant population show that ethnic identity is to a large degree socially constructed and consciously chosen. Feminism and feminist anthropology contribute to my understanding of Indian immigrant family life, gender roles and social activism.

Increasingly Indian immigrants, particularly women and younger people, are beginning to describe with great eloquence their own experiences as migrants in the U.S. The work of prize-winning author Bharat Mukherjee, poet/novelist Meena Alexander and filmmaker Mira Nair are already widely known. There are also large numbers of younger people whose work is appearing in such collections as *Our Feet Walk The Sky* (The Women of South Asian Descent Collective 1993) or Living in America (Rustomji-Kerns 1995). The question always arises of whether the outsider, in this case an American of Irish, English and French descent, can legitimately represent the experiences of South Asian new immigrants. I would argue that there is also validity in the outsider's view, especially when it is tempered with great admiration and respect for people courageous enough to leave old lives and to build new ones half a world away.

Indians In The New Migration

BEGINNINGS OF THE "NEW IMMIGRATION"

The year 1965 was a momentous one in recent United States history. In that year, Congress changed and liberalized laws governing immigration to this country. The resulting flow of newcomers—which added 6 million legal immigrants in the 1980s alone—has greatly changed the social profile of the American population. It has also profoundly affected the countries the immigrants left behind. In addition it has forced social scientists to think about immigrants and immigration in new ways.

The post-1965 wave of immigrants, often called the "new immigration," has profoundly reshaped the racial and ethnic composition of the U.S. population as millions of people, many of them of them from Asia, the Caribbean and Latin America, take up residence in a country dominated by people of European descent. The new immigration has enriched U.S. society by adding large numbers of ambitious, hard-working and often highly skilled new residents. It has also made the country's racial and ethnic composition more varied and complex and has given ethnicity—the sense of identity based on membership in a distinctive ethnic group—a new salience in American life.

At the same time, countries which send immigrants to the U.S. have also been deeply affected. On the one hand, they have often lost large numbers of their most educated and ambitious people to migration. On the other hand, these countries are now more intimately linked to the United States than before, since the new generation of immigrants has not abandoned contact with distant homelands. Telephones, faxes, videos and jet travel allow the new immigrants to stay in close touch with the people and places they left behind, in a way impossible to those earlier waves of migrants who reshaped American society in earlier generations.

The Asians among these new immigrants form a significant, fast-growing part of the new immigrant population. From China, Hong Kong, Japan, Korea, India, Pakistan, Bangladesh, Vietnam, Laos and the Philippines, in 1990 Asians made up 42 percent of all new immigrants (Gall and Gall 1993: 410). This book examines one of the larger Asian groups—people from India. Rather than surveying the entire Asian Indian population in the U.S., this book examines in detail the large Indian population which has settled in and around New York City.

New York City and its surrounding metropolitan areas have been a center of immigration for much of the last 200 years. By 1990, according to the U.S. census, New York City itself had 94,590 Indian residents (Doyle and Khandelwal 1994:1) while the larger metropolitan area (including New York City, adjacent counties in New York state, parts of New Jersey and Connecticut) had 199,010 Indian residents (Gall and Gall 1993: 679), almost a quarter of the 815,447 Indians in the U.S. at the time (Gall and Gall 1993: 569). Five years after the 1990 census, the Indian immigrant population in the U.S. was estimated to have grown to about one million. The largest concentrations of Indian immigrants live in California, New York, New Jersey, Illinois and Texas.

Most Asian Indians are new arrivals to the United States, born in India and living in this country no more than thirty years; in 1989, 70 percent of the Asian Indian population was foreign-born (Gall and Gall 1993:572). Furthermore this group continues to grow rapidly through further immigration. In 1991 alone, for instance, 45,064 Indian migrants entered the U.S. legally (Gall and Gall 1993: 412). In addition to this first generation there is a growing second generation, born to Indian parents but raised in this country.

The "new immigration" of which Asian Indians are a part is so called to distinguish it from that other period of massive, predominantly European "old immigration" which began in the mid-19th century, peaked in the early years of this century and lasted until the 1920s. In the 1920s for the first time immigration was sharply curtailed by law; the relatively small migration from Asia, already curbed by earlier laws, virtually ceased at that time. These immigration curbs were sparked by white Americans' increasing resentment toward immigrants and "foreigners," particularly those who were not white. Today the United States is again entering a period of anti-immigrant backlash, and there are new efforts to slow immigration (see Holmes 1995) as well as to encourage immigrants already here to leave.

The substantial changes in U.S. immigration laws in 1965 opened up Asian immigration by abandoning the national origins quota system which had favored northern and western Europeans. As a result Asians, who had been severely restricted in migrating, now had access to visas—with a limit of 20,000 per country—on the basis of labor market skills and family reunification. Particular kinds of educated, skilled or wealthy migrants were favored under the law and given preference in migrating. The law was a response to the U.S. economy's 20th century demands for a quick infusion of skilled workers and employment-generating investment. Additionally immigrants, once established as permanent residents, could sponsor the migration of their close relatives. Indians, like other Asian groups, quickly availed themselves of these new provisions.

For instance, from 1850 to 1960, only some 13,500 Indians had entered the U.S. legally (Gall and Gall 1993: 411). Some of these people were part of the "old" migration and had settled in northern California and the Pacific Northwest to work as farm laborers, mine workers, loggers or railway construction crews, alongside Chinese, Japanese and Filipino migrants (see Cheng and Bonacich 1984; Gibson 1988; Jensen 1988; La Brack 1988; Leonard 1992). Between 1961 and 1980, however, more than 191,000 Indian "new immigrants" had taken advantage of the changed laws to become U.S. residents. Some had come to find professional jobs or to start businesses; others came to join spouses, parents, siblings and children already here.

The new immigrants who have come to the U.S. since 1965 are different in many ways from the 19th century old immigrants with whom Americans were most familiar. Although there are still many refugees among them, fleeing political persecution, the new immigrants have, like their predecessors, come largely for economic reasons. What sets the new migrants apart is that large numbers are urban, middle class professionals and entrepreneurs. The newcomers are, overall, better educated and more highly skilled than their 19th century predecessors. Asian Indians are an especially skilled and well-educated group who arrive with high expectations of economic success.

In general Asians, particularly Indians, Koreans and Chinese, have been more successful economically than many other new immigrant groups; in certain areas they have even done better than the native-born population. For instance the 1980 U.S. Census indicates that while 24 percent of the white population held professional or managerial jobs, 47 percent of Asian Indians, 30 percent of the Chinese and 28 percent of the Japanese did so (Gall and Gall 1993:284). Indians are also proportionately more likely to own their own businesses (Gall and Gall 1993: 90). The U.S. Census reports that for 1990 almost 68 percent of the Indian immigrants who arrived in New York City before 1980 now have household incomes over $40,000 a year (quoted in City University of New York 1995: Table 3). This striking prosperity and professional success of the group as a whole has become a matter of great pride to Indian immigrant leaders and a central component of the ethnic group image they seek to create. It also means that those Indians who are unable to live up to this image, because they cannot find professional jobs or cannot earn much, are both humiliated, marginalized and sometimes exploited within their own ethnic population.

RACE, ETHNICITY OR PAN-ETHNICITY?

The other major difference between the old and new waves of U.S. migration lies in the realm of racial/ethnic categorization. The earlier migration was certainly heavily weighted towards whites of European background. In contrast, the contemporary newcomers are largely non-white. This means that new immigrants are, willingly or not, drawn into U.S. racial debates, as well as into debates about the role of immigrants in U.S. society. Not just cultural difference but race has made the new immigrants the target of contemporary xenophobia, discrimination and proposed new exclusionary laws.

This post-1965 infusion of people of color—Asians, Latin Americans and Caribbeans—has challenged existing American views on race and ethnicity (Alba 1990; Omi and Winant 1994). Many ordinary Americans once saw our population as polarized into two racial groups, a dominant group of whites and another, inferior group of blacks. The less numerous Hispanics, Native Americans and Asians were often lumped in some intermediate position, neither black nor white, less despised than African-Americans but less esteemed than whites—and still "a minority group." The model still tends to equate this racial/ethnic hierarchy with the class hierarchy, so that frequently discussions about "the poor" assume that all the poor are African-American, or at least non-white, and vice versa.

New immigrants of color have had to confront these hierarchies and racial/class stereotypes, whether they want to or not, and to position themselves accordingly (Jennings 1994; Marable 1994). First generation Indian immigrants, who are usually brown-skinned, with names, accents, body-language and dress which identify them as foreign, find it distressing and disorienting. In India they were neither "foreigners" nor "a minority group," were not poor and rarely faced discrimination. Here they have to deal with such categorization, and with the stigma which the term "minority" carries in American society. The dilemma does not wholly disappear for an Americanized Indian-American second generation, which is still marked by skin color and certain cultural differences.

Like other new immigrants, Asian Indians have had to find ways, individually and collectively, to insert themselves into the American racial hierarchy without accepting the stigmas involved. For many Indian immigrants and their children, ethnic group identity and ethnicity, have become the point of entry into U.S. society, and the vehicle for carving out a social role. Even this identity is not automatically assumed, however. When Indians first migrate to the U.S. they think of themselves as Indians living abroad, then begin to envision themselves as Americans. Very quickly, however, they realize that U.S. society divides itself along ethnic and racial lines. A great many Indian immigrants conclude that it is preferable to develop an ethnic group identity rather than accept a racial categorization. Furthermore, for many immigrants identity as part of an ethnic group permits them to stress their distinctive history, customs and culture; membership in a "racial minority" carries with it too much subtle stigma.

In creating a group identity, Indian immigrant leaders have emphasized very heavily Indian immigrants' prosperity, professional success and middle-class lifestyle. These class criteria are invoked to distance Indians from other groups of recent immigrants and from American-born minority groups as well as to suggest that Indians here are uniquely free from poverty, unemployment or such social problems as alcoholism, spouse abuse or divorce. In Indian-American thinking, such "shameful" personal or family problems are closely connected with failure and social marginality, and are thus something to be denied as bringing disgrace on the entire Indian immigrant population. Other Asian groups, which have experienced similar crises of self-identity, have labelled this the "model minority" myth.

Self-definitions beyond simple ethnic group identity are also available to Indian immigrants. For instance the category "Asian-American," which groups together people of Indian, Chinese, Korean, Vietnamese, Filipino or Japanese ancestry, offers Indians the potential for cross-ethnic alliances and delineation of common problems (Wei 1993). However, unlike other, longer-established Asian-American groups, the Indian immigrant population has been slow to embrace this form of pan-ethnic identity or to identify with other Asian groups

(Espiritu 1992). Some of the Indian immigrant concern to appear prosperous, middle-class and well-integrated into U.S. society may prevent Indians, particularly the self-appointed leaders of "the community," from forming such alliances with Asian-American groups, many of which have been vocal in contesting discrimination and racism. In explaining their reluctance to classify themselves as Asian-American, Indian immigrants emphasize the cultural differences which set them apart from Chinese, Koreans or Vietnamese immigrants.

A different outlook is emerging among members of the Indian second generation. Some of the children of Indian immigrants show a greater willingness to think of themselves as Asian-American as well as Indian- American. This has been accompanied, for some of the young, by a turn toward political activism (see Chapter 6) Younger people and intellectuals are more inclined to perceive all Asian immigrants as sharing a similar structural position in U.S. society, neither white nor black in racial terms but still subtly marginalized. Other young Indian-Americans seek a wider but less politicized identity as South Asians. They point to the common cultural heritage Indians share with other South Asians such as Bangladeshis, Sri Lankans and Pakistanis. This South Asian identity is more acceptable to the immigrant second generation than to their parents because the American-bred young are less preoccupied with historic religious antagonisms which divide India from Pakistan, Bangladesh and Sri Lanka.

DEVELOPING ETHNIC IDENTITY

Developing concepts of ethnic identity became easier for all new immigrants because the United States of the 1960s and 1970s was itself changing. The social movements of those decades challenged the old race-based hierarchies while suggesting that the U.S. could be multicultural without compromising its American identity. Partly in reaction to the African-American movement's philosophy of black pride, various white ethnic groups in the U.S. began to develop parallel concepts of ethnic pride. Long-established groups of Italian-Americans, Greek-Americans and Polish-Americans began to celebrate their ethnic distinctiveness rather than to stress their Americanization and assimilation. Amid the general liberalization of U.S. society at that period there was a growing interest in, and tolerance of, cultural differences. A vision of the U.S. as a multicultural society made up of ethnic groups, all equally important and legitimate, emerged as a new social model, partly—but not wholly—supplanting the older racial model.

Thus the first generation of post-1965 immigrants no longer finds itself, as 19th century immigrants had, under as much pressure from schools, social agencies, politicians and the media to assimilate quickly, to abandon "old-fashioned" language and customs, to feel ashamed of attachment to another culture, to become "real Americans" unmarked by ethnic identity. Greater ease of travel and communication have even allowed some new immigrants to become transnational—that is, to define themselves as simultaneous participants in both U.S. society and in the societies in which they were born (Schiller, Basch and Blanc-Szanton 1992: 1-24). Because of these shifts, many of the new immigrants have felt empowered to teach their children their mother tongues, to retain familiar customs, to celebrate their own ethnic heritage and to demand that others recognize it as well. Indian immigrants, like other groups arriving in the post-1965 period, participate in these processes involved in the creation of ethnic group identity.

This does not mean that racism, a dislike of foreigners and a rejection of social difference, of the kind that produced the earlier exclusionary immigration laws, have disappeared from American society. They are still very much present—even on the increase—and Indians, like other new immigrants, are often deeply shocked when they begin to understand the gulf between this country's official philosophy of ethnic pluralism and the actual prejudices which continue to operate. Some of the most difficult adjustments immigrants must make involve coming to terms with such contradictions. On a positive note, new immigrants are entering a society in which debate, protest and legal action against discrimination are more widespread and legitimate than they were 40 years ago. The present immigrant population has latitude, precedents and social support to oppose racism and discrimination actively.

THE INDIAN DIASPORA

The arrival of large numbers of Indian immigrants in the U.S. is not the first large-scale movement of migrants out of India. The 19th century was also marked by large flows of Indian immigrants to other countries, particularly to other parts of the British empire, creating what some Indians now call "the Indian diaspora." Today Indian immigrant leaders emphasize the continued connections between these diasporic populations scattered around the globe and India itself, invoking the history of past migration for political and economic ends.

Much of this earlier movement out of India also took the form of labor migration. Starting in the 1830s poor Indians were recruited as indentured laborers to the sugar plantations of the West Indies to replace African slave labor. Similar recruitment under British colonial sponsorship in the 19th and early 20th centuries later brought Indians to Fiji, Mauritius, Malaysia and Africa (Clarke, Peach and Vertovec 1990). By the end of the 19th century not all migrants went as laborers. Some went to provide services for sizeable Indian populations abroad. The young Mohandas Gandhi practiced law and political resistance in South Africa from 1893 until his return to India in 1915.

Today some of these Indo-Caribbeans or Indo-Africans have migrated again in the last 30 years to Britain, Canada and the U.S., partly as the result of ethnic conflict in their newly-independent countries. Today the presence of people Bhachu calls "twice-migrants" (1985) in the U.S., linked to, but not wholly part of the Indian-born migrant population, suggests the long history and the complexity of Indian migration. It also suggests the inadequacy of census categories based on race/ethnicity, since some of those who appear under the "Asian Indian" category in the U.S. are actually descendants of Indians who went to the Caribbean or Africa, and then re-migrated to the U.S. This group of Indo-Caribbeans and Indo-Africans is considered by immigrants from India to be Caribbean or African, on cultural grounds, rather than "real Indian." This group is thus not directly dealt with in this book. Nevertheless, their existence in New York on the fringes of the immigrant population from India is a useful reminder of India's long history of global migration. Today the Indian diaspora includes people of Indian descent who live not only in the U.S., Canada and Europe, but also Indians who live in the Middle East, in Southeast Asia and Latin America, the Caribbean and Africa.

As Indian immigrants begin to think of themselves as part of an historic process of migration, some of them develop concepts of pan-Indian identity, stressing cultural attributes India shares with its immigrant populations around the world. Other immigrants have begun to think about a "diasporic" identity, shared by Indians living outside of India.

THE POST-1965 ARRIVAL OF INDIANS IN THE U.S.

By the time the 1990 U.S. Census was conducted, the 815,562 people of "Asian Indian origin" resident here were outnumbered among the Asian population only by the Chinese, Filipino and Japanese immigrant populations. Because this is still a new immigrant population, most of those who list themselves on the census as Asian Indians are people born in India. Increasingly, however, their American-born children are becoming an important presence as college students and young professionals.

At present, the Indian immigrant population in the U.S. includes people from all parts India and from all caste groups. Nevertheless the largest concentrations come from north India, particularly from highly industrialized states such as Gujarat, Maharashtra or Uttar Pradesh (Saran and Eames 1980). Some come from states like the Punjab and Kerala which have long histories of labor migration. Indians in the U.S. are more likely to come from large cities and towns (which in the Indian context implies a certain modernity, sophistication and familiarity with English) and to be from middle and upper castes. Because of U.S. immigration requirements the primary migrants are generally people with some college education acquired either in India or in the U.S. A sizeable number arrived in the U.S. not only with college degrees but with postgraduate education or professional certification obtained in India. For instance in 1980, 87.3 percent of New York state's recently arrived Indians had completed high school and 60.8 percent had completed 4 or more years of college. Only Filipino immigrants had higher educational levels (Youssef 1992:93). In India only a tiny proportion of the population has the opportunity to study beyond high school.

Their education immediately identifies Indian immigrants as relatively privileged in their own country, since so much of India is still rural and most people are employed in agriculture. Illiteracy rates are high (40-60 percent) even in cities and women are more likely to be illiterate than men. Unlike the U.S., where college education is widely available, only a small fraction of Indians, probably less than 10 percent, have access to highly competitive Indian universities or to specialized training. Thus, although India is an extremely poor country, it is not its poorest citizens who migrate to the U.S., but rather its most sophisticated: people trained in economics, medicine, nursing, engineering or management. Ambitious middle-class people from professional families leave for the West in search of careers they cannot find at home.

Understandably, India, like many other underdeveloped countries with large out-migration, is worried about this "brain drain," which deprives it of the very people needed to speed development (Bhagwati 1976). Many Indian migrants are aware of this dilemma. While some come to this country eagerly, full of enthusiasm and anticipation, others come more reluctantly, guilty about abandoning family and country but despairing of any chance to better themselves if they remain. The warring emotions of ambition, nostalgia and Indian patriotism make virtually every Indian immigrant ambivalent at times about his or her decision to leave India.

THE IMPORTANCE OF THE JOB

The primary Indian immigrants—that is, those who are the first in their families to enter the U.S. on student or labor certification visas—are likely to be men ranging from their twenties to their early thirties (Gall and Gall 1993: 417-418). Once established, these primary immigrants hasten to sponsor the migration of wives and children, and eventually of siblings and parents as well. This pattern reflects Indian society's emphasis on marriage and family solidarity, an emphasis which remains strong among Indian immigrants here. Relatively few women come to the U.S. as primary migrants—most arrive to join husbands, fathers, brothers or children—since Indian culture restricts women's autonomy to seek careers and to travel independently. That so many Indian immigrant women have arrived as the spouses of male migrants not only reflects traditional gender roles prevalent in India but may help perpetuate such roles among immigrants here.

Still, some Indian women do come to the U.S. alone as students, particularly in the sciences. In addition, during the U.S. nursing shortages of the 1970s and 1980s, many female nurses (Reimers 1992: 101) came to work in U.S. hospitals, alongside Filipinas and Caribbean women. Many of the Indian nurses come from the state of Kerala, an area which has traditionally given women somewhat more independence than the rest of India.

On arrival the first task for most Indian men is to find work or to get further training which will lead to work. Those who come on student visas look for jobs here after graduation. They seek employers who will sponsor them for permanent residence. Women, unless they are the primary migrants or have advanced professional training, may be slower to enter the work force. One of the attractions of the U.S., and of New York City in particular, is the availability of relatively inexpensive public higher education and technical training. This public higher education has played an historic role since the earlier part of this century in funneling generations of immigrants and their children into the U.S. professional middle class. Today the new immigrants and their children fill the classrooms of city colleges and universities. They are particularly drawn to courses of study which seem to be most directly related to employment: science, computing, business and finance, law, medicine and medical technology. This route to employment and economic assimilation is now threatened; proposed legislation in New York restricting the right of immigrants to certain public benefits might also deny many college students this kind of low-cost education.

Indian immigrants clearly recognize that a good professional job or a flourishing business of one's own is the single most important factor in achieving the rewards of migration: a house, a car, a good education for the children, nice furniture and household equipment, enough money to help relatives back in India. Work, money and the prestige they bring are central concerns. As one immigrant remarked, "Things are different here. Nobody cares who your father was or where you were born. Not like India. Here all they care about is how well you do your job and how much you earn. That's it."

Except for the relatively few graduates from India's premier scientific training institutes, directly recruited to work in U.S. firms, or nurses hired by particular hospitals, most Indians do not arrive with jobs awaiting them. They must prepare resumes, comb the newspaper help wanted ads and visit employment bureaus. They rely heavily on advice and contacts provided by fellow immigrants who have lived here longer. Those who plan to start their own businesses have to research the U.S. business climate, decide where to locate, what they will sell, whether their primary market will be Americans or fellow Indians, and how to deal with an American work force. Like other entrepreneurs, they embark on a search for credit, investment partners and whatever government assistance is available.

As a group, Indian immigrants have tended to be successful in finding both careers and good incomes via work in medical fields, in scientific research or teaching, in engineering, computing, insurance, banking and finance. Others have become successful entrepreneurs running businesses which range from small, family-run shops to large manufacturing firms and international investment corporations.

Overall this is an immigrant group whose education, hard work and ambition have boosted them to middle- or upper-middle class status within U.S. society. There is, however, a sector of the Indian population which has been less successful. Although employed, these immigrants tend to have mundane or even menial jobs which bring neither wealth nor prestige. There is considerable debate among Indian immigrants themselves about who these people are and how they came to be here. Successful Indians tend to regard these less successful fellow immigrants as something of an embarrassment to a group proud of its wealth and success.

Some observers assume that these poor Indians, such a contrast to the boasted prosperity of the group as a whole, are simply less qualified people who somehow won residence in the U.S. because they were sponsored by their professional relatives (Visaria and Visaria 1990). One Indian immigrant leader remarked contemptuously that "These fellows are our stupider brothers and cousins" and insisted that they were in no way representative. This viewpoint tends to blame the unfortunate worker and to ignore such factors as discrimination, a mismatch between immigrants' training and available employment, and an intensifying recession in the U.S. economy since the late 1980s. This recession has reached into the ranks of young science professionals, creating un- and underemployment among them (Browne 1995:16).

Although research on this poorer sector of the Indian immigrant population is badly needed, observation suggests that many of these immigrants are urban and middle class in origin, not unlike their more successful compatriots. Some arrived in the U.S. with only a high-school education and have become trapped in poorly-paid or low-status work here because a college degree is a prerequisite for a "good" job. Some are actually college graduates who have nevertheless experienced downward social mobility into the U.S. working class because their Indian training is deemed inappropriate for American professional employment (Lessinger 1990). Still others are struggling petty shopkeepers who have been unable to build a small, family-run store into a larger, more profitable enterprise.

Virtually all such Indian immigrants are shocked to find that their training and middle-class backgrounds are insufficient to insert them into professional positions. A relatively small number have entered the U.S. without valid visas, hoping to find work "off the books" until they can arrange a legal way to stay on. Like other undocumented workers, such people are employed but are particularly vulnerable to exploitation, afraid to demand better pay, better working conditions and benefits for fear of deportation.

CULTURAL ADVANTAGES

Although successful Indian immigrants usually attribute their success in the American job market to their individual virtues of courage, hard work, frugality and family loyalty, this is only part of the picture. Equally important are the skills and advantages they enjoy, derived both from their middle-class backgrounds in India and from India's colonial history.

The most striking advantage Indian immigrants bring with them is fluency in English. After 200 years under British colonial domination, India's urban middle class values higher education as a route to social mobility. This class also speaks, reads and writes English and is usually educated in Western-style schools where books and teaching continue to be in English and the curriculum is either British or American in structure. This gives urban, middle-class Indians privileged access to the international worlds of science, technology, finance and management, whose common language across national borders is now English. It also means that almost 45 percent of Indian immigrants here use English even at home (Gall and Gall 1993: 128).

Fluency in spoken and written English means that Indian immigrants have a clear advantage on arrival here when compared, for instance, to equally well- educated middle-class Korean, Russian or Haitian immigrants. The Indian with a degree in chemistry does not have to struggle to learn English before enrolling in a U.S. graduate program or finding a job; indeed the Indian's qualifications, derived from a familiar educational system, are often given greater weight and recognition by American employers.

The other advantage Indian immigrants have is one which sets them apart from many native-born Americans: the ability to mobilize investment capital through family networks. This does not mean Indian immigrants come from very rich families. Most do not. Indeed Indian salaries and savings are tiny when translated into American dollars. A well-paid Indian professional, for instance, might earn the equivalent of $200-600 a month. Yet Indian immigrants use a cultural pattern which mobilizes contributions from a wide family network for investments seen as beneficial to the entire family.

The would-be immigrant who needs money for a ticket to the U.S. or the established immigrant who wants to start a business or buy property here calls on relatives and close friends, in the U.S. and in India, for interest-free loans. Because those involved are middle class, they have resources to contribute: a piece of jewelry to sell, property to mortgage, a pension plan to cash in. When combined and pooled, these contributions give the immigrant enough to start out. If the venture succeeds, the relatives and friends not only get their loans repaid but expect reciprocal kinds of assistance. For instance the sister who sells her bracelets to buy her brother an airplane ticket to the U.S. probably expects that brother, once settled abroad, to help her own son get admitted to an engineering program in an American university.

Indians are not the only immigrants with these kinds of family patterns which mobilize resources. Korean and Chinese immigrants in particular also draw on family and community loyalties to pool money used to capitalize business and investment (Martin 1993: A1, B6). Because the use of family networks to generate business capital is less prevalent among native-born Americans, whose family relationships tend to be more individualistic, it is a poorly understood aspect of Asian immigrant life. Asians are sometimes the object of envy and suspicion here. Non-immigrant neighbors wonder where Asians got the money to buy a house or open a factory so soon after arrival in the U.S.; there are ugly rumors about illicit sources of funding. Asians' business and professional achievements also take on a political dimension when conservative U.S. politicians reproach American-born African-Americans and Hispanics for their failure to become successful entrepreneurs like new Asian immigrants, ignoring the different cultural, class and economic resources each group brings to the situation.

Some Asian-American activists now argue that the "myth of the 'model minority,'" which defines Asian-Americans as uniformly successful, well-to-do and free of social problems, actually victimizes Asian-Americans. The myth denies and obscures the kinds of poverty, discrimination and racism Asians actually face in the U.S. (Kwong 1987; Takaki 1989; Omatsu 1994). When an ethnic group itself subscribes to the myth of its own success, as Indian immigrants do, organizing to remedy problems is all the more difficult.

WHY CHOOSE NEW YORK CITY?

Given Indian immigrants' focus on professional or entrepreneurial careers, it is not surprising that so many of them— 199,010 according to the 1990 census—have opted to settle in New York City and its surrounding residential suburbs. Today New York City outranks Chicago, Los Angeles or Houston as a center of Indian immigration. Some 16 percent of just-arrived Indians told the Immigration and Naturalization Service in 1991 that they intended to settle in New York City (Gall and Gall 1993: 425). Although New York's urban congestion and fast pace may frighten some immigrants (not to mention many American suburbanites), big, bustling, dirty cities hold no terrors for urban Indians. Instead New York offers housing (New York's notorious high rents have their parallel in most Indian cities), low-cost education, a certain racial tolerance and above all—work. New York's mixed economy offers a great variety of the kinds of jobs Indians want. Although some Indians come to the New York area because they have relatives or friends already settled there, most head for the region primarily because its employment advantages are already well-know among those preparing to migrate.

Industries in nearby New Jersey and Connecticut and upstate New York, as well as in the city itself, hire Indian engineers, while computer firms want Indian software designers. Scientific employers claim that young Indian scientists are often brighter, better-prepared and more hardworking than their American counterparts. (The young Indian employees are sometimes bitter to find they have been offered lower salaries than American coworkers; employers often assume immigrants will accept any job offered them.)

New York's numerous hotels and motels offer Indians both jobs and chances to invest. The city's banking, insurance and finance industry hires Indians; its enormous public health system needs Indian doctors, nurses, pharmacists, anesthesiologists and accountants. The city and state bureaucracies hire Indians as clerks, managers and administrators. Indians are found on the faculties of the city's universities and medical schools. New York, with its large garment and jewelry sectors, makes room for Indian importer/manufacturers of textiles, clothing, leather garments and gemstones.

In addition, New York City has historically shunned malls and megastores in favor of small, local, family-run retail stores. Previous generations of European immigrants have supported themselves and their families through such shops. Indians in their turn now use family labor to operate Hallmark card shops, newsstands and candy stores, grocery stores and delicatessens, clothing boutiques, health food shops, gas stations and muffler repair shops, restaurants and coffee shops. With the growth of a large Indian population in New York, there is now scope for many entrepreneurs who sell almost entirely to fellow Indians.

The other kind of benefit New York City offers Indian immigrants is a large labor market for unskilled workers. Within a heavily professional ethnic group, there are, as noted earlier, a number of Indians who do not fit the mold and cannot find the stable, middle-class jobs they dreamed of before migration. While for some the failure to find professional work can be offset through entrepreneurship, other people are obliged to work for wages—often very low wages. Although New York City has lost much of its manufacturing base since the early part of this century, when thousands of small industries employed hundreds of thousands of unskilled and semi-skilled immigrant workers, some manufacturing does remain. Additionally there is a great deal of work available in the service sector.

Indian immigrants, including college graduates, work as waiters, deli countermen, shop clerks, newsstand employees, security guards or taxi drivers. Those who work for fellow Indians as waiters, hotel night clerks, shop assistants or domestic servants often do so under very exploitative conditions (Lessinger 1992; Melwani 1995). Indians who do such work live out an immigrant experience far closer to that of poor Dominican, Chinese or Mexican immigrants than to that of fellow Indians.

Indians holding such low status jobs are often deeply ashamed of their lack of success. Their shame is often intensified by the very high aspirations with which they arrived in the U.S. as well as by the proud self-image of Indian immigrants as a group. Nevertheless, in New York such service workers do have a niche, a way to survive, if only marginally, until (with luck) something better turns up. It is important that their stories, too, be included in any account of Indian immigration.

Finally, it is important to note the ways in which New York's multi-ethnic character, product of almost 200 years of immigration, affects Indian immigrants' development of an ethnic identity. New York probably contains members of more different ethnic groups than any other city in the United States; more than a quarter of its population is now foreign-born. The heterogeneity of the population has often led to political tension and inter-ethnic competition. Typically, longer-established ethnic groups have resented the arrival of newcomers who appear to be ruining the neighborhood and soaking up an unfair share of social services. However at an official level New York prides itself on being "a city of immigrants" or a "glorious mosaic" and conceptualizes its population as made up of numerous equal, if competing, ethnic groups.

For Indian immigrants who move to New York, this means two things. On the one hand, they report somewhat lower levels of racial prejudice and anti-foreign discrimination than Indians find in other parts of the U.S. On the other hand there are active official efforts to incorporate them as a group into the city's fabric. A business executive who came to the U.S. as a student and then worked as an engineer in an automobile plant in Illinois spoke, rather reluctantly, about the discrimination he had faced there. When he moved to New York, he recalled, people paid much less attention to his dark skin and his accent and seemed to accept him for what he could do. Some Indians even joke about the meaning of "American" identity amidst New York's ethnic variety. A man said, "When I first got here, I looked around me. Everywhere I saw Puerto Ricans, people from Korea, Jamaicans, Ethiopians. Even some Russians. I asked my friend, 'Where are the Americans? *Who* are the Americans?'"

As a way to bridge the divisions within its wildly varied population, New York City officials, cultural leaders and social service agencies actively promote festivals and events intended to foster ethnic pride and to glorify the city's multiethnic character. Immigrant populations are encouraged to take part in street fairs, parades, public religious festivals, exhibits in local museums and libraries, school programs featuring students' ethnic heritages, culture, dance and food festivals. All drive home to new immigrants the fact that ethnic identity is simultaneously something to be proud of and a social base within the urban environment. New York's Indian immigrants are thus constantly engaged in an ongoing process of creating themselves as Indian-Americans, or even as Indian-American New Yorkers. This process is occurring in parallel, although perhaps not identical, ways in other areas of the U.S. where large numbers of Indians have settled.

MOVING OUT TO SUBURBIA

Although New York City remains the economic and cultural center of Indian immigrant life in the New York area, there are many Indian immigrants who have moved out of the city, into surrounding suburbs. Increasing, some of these immigrants move directly to suburban areas such as New Jersey. The move to outlying suburbs is sometimes to find work, more often to find nice apartments or houses for sale in quiet middle- or upper-middle-class neighborhoods. Like other middle-class Americans, Indians are looking for a quiet, crime-free life with space, greenery and clean, modern housing and decent schools. In the last decade a parallel kind of suburbanization has been taking place in India, where the middle class has moved to the outskirts of major cities to find modern housing and to escape congestion, pollution and water shortages in old inner cities. Much of that new housing in Indian cities is now built to look American, a reminder of the ways Indian immigrants' consumer tastes now influence India.

The desire to become home-owners is a major reason why Indians in the New York area choose to live in the suburbs. As in India, ownership of one's own home is vital in establishing middle-class status and providing family security. Thus many Indians have been drawn to boroughs of New York City— Queens, Brooklyn, or the Bronx—where one- or two-family houses are available. Many people eventually decide that they can buy a bigger, more modern house for the same money by leaving the city altogether. They move to Long Island or Westchester County, or to suburban towns in Connecticut or New Jersey, often while continuing to work in New York City itself. With the relocation of certain businesses out of the city to Westchester or New Jersey, Indians may also move to find employment.

In the United States, the quality of local public schools is also a major factor in Indian immigrants' movement to suburbia. Indian immigrants are highly ambitious for their children. They are deeply concerned that their children receive good educations in preparation for secure, well-paid and prestigious professional jobs. In India acceptable primary and secondary education is only available through expensive, competitive private schools, the stepping-stone to elite universities. Once in New York many parents realize that the schools in more affluent suburban communities are most like elite Indian schools, with better facilities, smaller classes and more rigorous academic programs than the average crowded, underfunded New York City public school.

In discussing such issues, Indian immigrant parents also voice a certain amount of prejudice absorbed from their new society (but rooted in similar classcaste prejudices common in India). "Perhaps it is racist to say it," explained one parent defiantly, "but I will **not** have my child hanging out with those ignorant kids who never want to study at all." By "those ignorant kids" this father meant his daughter's African-American and Hispanic classmates. However the flight to the suburbs does not always protect Indian immigrants from issues of race. Teachers on Long Island report the constant discussions about racial identity which go on among their Asian students. Many young Indian-American students express puzzlement about whether they are white or black, say their teachers.

Consider the cases of two families who moved out of New York City proper to suburbia. The cases show why Indians of different class background are attracted to the suburbs, as well as some of the ways in which relatives offer each other economic support after migration. In the first case a family has moved from Queens, the New York City borough with the largest concentration of Indians, to an affluent suburb in the greater New York metropolitan area. In the second case a family has moved from Queens to a working-class/lower-middle-class suburban town in New Jersey which remains within commuting distance of New York City.

Mr. Lal, who has been in the U.S. for 28 years, told me about his successive moves which paralleled the growth of his family and his increasing prosperity. As a student he shared a cheap room in a decrepit residential hotel in Manhattan's Upper West Side with another Indian student. When he finished college and was able to sponsor his wife's migration, the couple rented an inexpensive three-room apartment in the New York City borough of Queens. Mr. Lal went to work as an engineer in a small Manhattan firm while his wife stayed home to raise the children. At the time Queens was beginning to attract immigrants of all kinds, who found relatively inexpensive housing and relatively safe neighborhoods there.

In Queens the family saved every penny they could, buying minimal furniture, wearing their oldest clothes at home, eating simple, largely vegetarian food, avoiding any entertainment that cost money. This austere life-style is a pattern which one rich Indian called "living like a mouse in a hole." It is typical of many newly arrived Indian immigrants anxious to accumulate savings. It formed the basis of the Lals' present visible prosperity.

After a number of years the Lals had enough to buy a car and a small house in a suburban town on Long Island, to the east of New York City, and moved there with their two small children. The move was partially to obtain a more prestigious address and a better house. Mr. Lal continued to work in New York City, and his colleagues often made disparaging remarks about Queens and its (supposed) lower-middle-class character. An apartment in the basement of the Long Island house, rented to another Indian, helped pay the mortgage.

When their oldest child was in fourth grade, the family moved again to another, more affluent Long Island community known for its fine schools. The house they bought was bigger and considerably more elegant, and they have furnished it with a certain ostentation. Mr. Lal proudly shows first-time visitors a small prayer room he had constructed in an alcove off the dining room. Because there was no attached apartment to rent out, Mrs. Lal went to work as the bookkeeper for a medical group to help pay for the house and furniture. This required the purchase of a second car.

Now that the family has plenty of space, they entertain often. Mr. Lal's parents visit regularly from India and stay with him for several months each summer. He has sponsored the immigration of two of his brothers, who lived with the Lals until they got married. Both still live nearby. Because of its excellent schools the area has become very popular with Indian, Korean and Chinese immigrants; house prices have risen sharply. In order to keep them nearby, Mr. Lal had to subsidize both his brothers when they bought their houses.

In contrast, the Verma brothers have managed to buy a house despite relatively low wages by sharing a household and pooling both incomes and expenses (see Garner, Robey and Smith 1985: 34-35). The brothers came to the U.S. in 1985 and lived with distant cousins in Queens while looking for work. The older brother helped his cousin run a small grocery store in Queens while the younger brother got night work tending a 24-hour newsstand. Both brothers earned very low hourly wages. Things began to get tense in the household where five adults and three children shared four small rooms. Part of the tension was also over finances. Both brothers were trying to save money. The cousins, initially welcoming, began to demand contributions for rent and food which, the brothers thought, were exorbitant. (In fact the cousins were themselves struggling to make ends meet and could not afford to feed two extra adults indefinitely. Traditional Indian hospitality to family members undergoes strain in immigrants' new circumstances.)

Eventually both Vermas found jobs in a New Jersey factory through a fellow Indian who already worked there. The wages were modest but the jobs had regular hours and offered benefits. The brothers moved to a shabby but cheap rented apartment not far from the factory as a prelude to sponsoring their wives' migration from India. Today the brothers and their wives and children live in a house they bought together in a working-class suburb near the factory. The downstairs apartment is rented to nonIndian tenants. One brother continues to work as a factory supervisor while the other has saved enough to lease his own news stand in the New York City subway.

The wife of the younger Verma brother works as a clerk in a convenience store. The older Mrs. Verma sometimes helps in her husband's news stand but primarily runs the joint household and looks after her two children and her sister-in-law's one child. The two Verma brothers are content with the shared household, which has prospered because it contains three wage-earners. The women, however, would like separate establishments and talk about asking the tenant to leave. The younger Mrs. Verma in particular resents her sister-in- law's control over the kitchen, although she acknowledges that she could not keep her job, which she likes if the older woman did not watch her child and do much of the cooking.

With more limited aspirations than the Lals, the Vermas are content with the quality of the local public schools, although concerned about the racial animosity their children face from white and Hispanic teenagers in the neighborhood.

The movement out of New York City to the suburbs has dispersed the Indian immigrant population and prevented the formation of large Indian residential enclaves. Although neighborhoods in Queens and Brooklyn, and New Jersey towns like Jersey City or Edison have significant Indian populations, Indians are never the single, dominant ethnic group. This, along with economic integration via jobs in American firms and institutions, means that most Indian immigrants necessarily live in a multi-ethnic setting once they move beyond the household and circle of kin and friends. They are less able than some immigrant groups to retreat into a world made up entirely of fellow ethnics.

Indian immigrant cultural identity is therefore largely defined through activities like consumption, the display of badges of Indian identity like traditional dress, or participation in Indian cultural and religious organizations. It is further defined through active participation in networks of kin and friends which stretch across the U.S., back to India, and into countries like Canada, Britain or Australia where Indian immigrants have settled.

It is tempting to look at the Lals and the Vermas, or at Indian-born immigrant parents and their American-born children, and to see one group as "more assimilated" than the other. However in this book I avoid the older concepts of assimilation such as those that spoke of the U.S. as a "melting pot." Instead I prefer to talk about the creation of identity among immigrants. Rather than asking "How Indian do these immigrants remain?" or "How American have they become?" or "How have they assimilated?" I focus on some of the ways Indians come to construct new identities for themselves from their experiences as migrants.

Upon arrival here, Indians are already a diverse and internally differentiated immigrant population (Fisher 1980; Helweg and Helweg 1990). India itself is large and culturally very diverse, with many distinct regional cultures, languages and religions. India's population is further stratified by both caste and class. Much of India's internal diversity is reproduced among Indian immigrants, so that those coming to the U.S. speak different languages, bring with them different kinds of experiences and regional cultures, come from slightly different class backgrounds and move into a variety of social settings in this country. Out of these diversities Indians construct their identities in the U.S.

Once established, Indians develop identities which are complex and many-layered. People may think of themselves—depending on context—as Indian immigrants, or as Indian-Americans, or Americans of South Asian descent, as Asians or simply as Americans. At the same time they may also think of themselves as exporters or doctors, speakers of Tamil or Gujarati, as community activists, as members of the

middle class, as devout Hindus or Muslims, or as housewives, community activists, suburbanites or Republicans.
Furthermore these constellations of identities may change
over time. Indian immigrants themselves are acutely aware
of the differences created simply by length of residence in the
U.S. and talk frequently about the differences between the
first and second immigrant generations.

This internal differentiation is one reason why I avoid re-
ferring to Indian immigrants as a "community." Indian immigrant leaders use the term frequently, and when writing or
speaking publicly will refer to "the community," implying
that fellow immigrants from India form a single, unified and
undifferentiated group. Often these leaders contrast "the
community" with "the Americans," implying a we-they distinction. On examination, however, Indian immigrants in the
U.S. rarely act as a single community. The population is too
diverse, too spread out geographically, to do so. Indian leaders' discourse about "the Indian community" and search for
common symbols of Indian-ness are part of their effort to construct an ethnic group and an ethnic identity (Lessinger 1993).

Creating Ethnic Identity

THE STRUCTURES OF EVERYDAY LIFE

If there is no single Indian immigrant community, there are nevertheless institutions and activities which provide a framework for many Indians' lives here. Full of meaning, these institutions and activities penetrate daily life and become part of people's vision of what it means to be Indian in New York. Things such as the purchase and consumption of culturally marked goods and services, cycles of religious worship, attendance at public festivals celebrating Indian identity and relying on the Indian immigrant media are part of how Indians constitute themselves an ethnic group and part of the self-representation by which they interact with other groups.

This does not mean that such activities replace for Indian immigrants a daily life of work, school, shopping and socializing, all of which involve interaction with American society. Nor does it mean every immigrant from India takes part in all of these activities all of the time. The secular may rarely visit religious institutions. People may shop in Indian stores only a few times a year. The intellectuals may scorn public festivals or glance only occasionally at the local Indian immigrant media. Yet all are acutely aware of Indian institutions and activities and the extent to which they signify "Indian-ness." By looking at some of these activities in detail, a clear picture emerges of the cultural patterns which Indian immigrants value and try to live by, or conversely, react against.

NEW YORK'S "LITTLE INDIA"—A SYMBOLIC CENTER

The symbolic heart of the Indian population in New York City is at present the Indian shopping area in the Jackson Heights area of Queens. This "Little India" at 74th Street and 37th Avenue, at the junction of two subway lines, is one of the many areas of Queens revived since the 1960s by the influx of large numbers of new immigrants. The borough of Queens was home 56,601 Indians in 1990—the single largest concentration of Indians in the city (Doyle and Khandelwal 1994:2)—so it is not surprising that the largest Indian shopping area is located there as well.

Walking down 74th Street on a Saturday, visitors might easily believe they have strayed out of a familiar American city and into a modern shopping area in urban India, so reminiscent are the sights, sounds and smells. Although there are other concentrations of Indian shops elsewhere in greater New York, including one on Lexington Avenue in Manhattan and another in Edison, New Jersey, this area in is Queens the largest and busiest, the one its users say "reminds us of home."

In the absence of clearly-defined Indian immigrant residential enclaves, this "Little India" offers a focus and center to a population geographically dispersed throughout the greater metropolitan area by regularly concentrating large numbers of Indians in one place as shopkeepers, employees and customers. Khandelwal calls it one of the "core areas" of New York City's Indian population (1995: 186-188).

The sense of stepping into the middle of another culture one encounters on 74th Street is familiar to New Yorkers, and indeed to the residents of many large American cities. All over the U.S., wherever immigrants have settled in large numbers, concentrations of ethnic shops such as this one have sprung up in urban neighborhoods. Little Italys, Chinatowns, Little Havanas or Little Odessas develop as centers of local Italian, Chinese, Cuban or Russian immigrant culture. Unlike New York's Chinatowns, however, Little India is not simultaneously an Indian residential community. Instead the area serves a dispersed Indian population which arrives by subway or car from all over the metropolitan area. Indeed many of these shops also serve Indians all over the U.S. through their mail-order services which ship goods to people living beyond New York's commercial hub (Khandelwal 1995: 191).

Ethnic shopping enclaves themselves play an important role in New York's economy. For instance the commercial growth and bustle of 74th Street has revitalized a once-depressed Queens commercial area. The entrepreneurial drive and skill for which Indian immigrants are becoming known means Indian businesses now compete to lease or buy shops in an area which in the 1970s, under nonIndian proprietorship, featured greasy luncheonettes, vacant stores and a pornographic movie house. The investment of Indian immigrant capital and hard work has transformed the area and has generated employment for fellow Indians who work in the area's shops and restaurants or who supply the retail stores.

On nearby blocks Chinese, Koreans, Greeks and Colombians with equal commercial flair have reclaimed other streets in similar fashion. Older residents sometimes complain about "the changing neighborhood;" Queens, which was 78 percent white in 1970 had become 48 percent white, 20 percent black, 20 percent Hispanic and 12 percent Asian by 1990 (New York City Planning Department figures quoted in Firestone 1995: B1, B4). Yet Queens is now a thriving borough as a result of the influx of new immigrants, who have replaced an older white population which has left for the suburbs.

A careful look at the shoppers and the shops of Little India reveals a great deal about Indian immigrant values, sense of self, adaptations, relationship to U.S. society and ongoing connection with the far-off country that was once home. It also makes visible a number of the other themes which will be elaborated in this and succeeding chapters: the importance of family; gender roles; the transnational character of the Indian immigrant population; questions of status and class difference within a single ethnic population; the sense of unease many Indian immigrants still feel in this society, and differences in outlook between the immigrant first generation and the American-raised second generation. Virtually all of what is sold on 74th Street is symbolic of Indian-ness, things largely first-generation immigrants feel embody and sum up a cultural identity of which they are very proud. The previous chapter pointed out that ethnic identity is both actively created and publicly demonstrated. Consumption is part of that process. Like other comparable immigrant shopping enclaves, Little India exists to provide the kinds of things—at once utilitarian and badges of ethnicity—which immigrants cannot find in their own neighborhoods or local shopping malls.

Indian Americans in New York and its surrounding suburbs boast to their relatives visiting from India, "Whatever you can buy in New Delhi, you can also buy on 74th Street." This is not quite true, but nevertheless the area's range of goods and services permit first generation immigrants to recreate significant aspects of Indian life in an American context. The area will undoubtedly evolve and change character as Indian immigrants' American-born children grow up and establish families, with their own definitions of what it means to be Indian-American. Already, however, Little India has something for them as well.

Part of 74th Street's appeal to its shoppers is variety: Indian groceries, restaurants and sweet shops, a travel agency, an astrologer, a package shipping service, a tailor. Shops sell Indian clothing, religious items, jewelry, sandals, Indian cosmetics and home remedies, tapes and videos, kitchen equipment, Indian or Indian immigrant newspapers, books and magazines. Some shops sell tickets to Indian cultural events: concerts, dance-drama performances, plays, poetry readings, or the song-and-dance revues featuring visiting Indian movie stars. As Khandelwal notes, some of these shops, particularly grocery stores, acknowledge a common South Asian identity-through-consumption by announcing that they sell "Indo-Pak-Bangla" goods (1995: 191).

Although many of the shoppers think of their consumption as maintaining an Indian way of life, it would be a mistake to imagine that these immigrants are simply reproducing "traditional India" in America. Indian immigrants pride themselves on their ability to combine tradition with modernity and innovation. They believe in the value of higher education, demand as much of it as possible for their children, and deeply respect those with advanced degrees and technical expertise. Many are well-traveled, since they visit relatives spread out around the globe. They have an easy familiarity with advanced technology and use it extensively. Many follow world events closely, particularly those affecting India. Their children keep up with international trends in fashion and popular music. This modern, flexible, global outlook is visible in Little India alongside tradition.

STREET SCENE

On a weekend along 74th Street entire family groups, laden with packages, can be seen moving in and out of stores from which come strains of Indian music and the smell of spices. An elderly man in a turban passes out leaflets advertising the services of a newly-opened tailoring business. Suited businessmen stand chatting by the doors of restaurants. Many shop windows and doorways carry posters for classical or pop concerts and dance performances that are organized by New York-area Indian cultural associations or are put together by those Indian-American businessmen who double as promoters for particular shows. The businessmen expect profit from the performances plus publicity and status from linking their names to the glamour of the film or music world.

Women with babies in strollers sip tea in a sweet and snack shop after serious shopping. Some of the ladies wait for fresh rounds of flat bread to come out of the deep oven. Others choose bright pink, green, yellow or orange sweets, made from milk, nuts, butter and sugar, to go with their tea. At another table taxi drivers are taking a break and discussing an issue of *India Abroad*, one of the local Indian immigrant newspapers. Their conversation ranges from the scores in a recent India-Pakistan cricket match to lurid details of a local embezzlement scandal. In the back of the store a man is conferring with the manager, placing an order for many pounds of sweets to be delivered to his home next day. His son has just been admitted to Harvard, and the family plans to celebrate by distributing boxes of the elaborate, silver-decorated confections to family and friends to symbolize the sharing of joy and good fortune.

Between the jewelry store and the electronics shop a security guard paces back and forth, scanning the dense crowd. The street's merchant association has hired the guard after a series of purse snatchings and car break-ins carried out by youthful, non-Indian thugs. Merchants explain that many of their customers are suburbanites, elderly people or visitors on holiday from India; all are less street-wise and wary than long-time New Yorkers. Furthermore, many shoppers are carrying a good deal of cash since people tend to come to Little India to make large purchases. The merchants meet regularly with the local police precinct in an effort to keep foot and car patrols attentive to the area.

Further along 74th Street teenagers in sweatshirts, baggy or ultra-tight jeans and rakish haircuts gather in a video and music store to pore over a new tape by the Indo-British rap artist who calls himself Apache Indian. In the back of the same video store grandmothers wearing saris and woolen shawls debate whether to rent some episodes of the Hindu religious epic "The Mahabharata" or a copy of the newest blockbuster movie from Bombay, center of India's film industry. The old ladies decide on "Hum Aapke Hain Koun?" (What Am I to You?), a newly released Bombay film with a convoluted plot about a man who ends up with two wives. It is advertised as full of family values and wonderful songs.

CONSUMPTION AND ETHNIC IDENTITY

Like all recent immigrants, Indians remain emotionally attached to the food, clothing, music and language they grew up with. Such things remain a powerful reminder of "home" and become even more intensely important to immigrants as the visible signs of ethnic identity. Indians are aware of popular American stereotypes about India as a hopelessly poor and backward country; it embarrasses and irritates them, since most still feel great loyalty to India. They feel obliged to demonstrate that they come from a large, important country with its own long history, vibrant culture and well-developed aesthetic sense.

While living among American neighbors and spending their days among American coworkers and friends, most Indians still try to eat Indian food regularly, wear Indian dress on important occasions, participate in Indian cultural events, and most importantly, maintain close contact with extended family. It is no surprise, therefore, that Indian shopping areas always feature the cluster of stores which Indians themselves refer to sarcastically as "The Big Three": grocery and spice shops, sari/jewelry shops and electronic goods stores. All are central to what most Indians here would define as "our Indian way of life."

Like all ethnic groups, Indians define themselves partly by their cuisine. The grocery and spice shops provide Indian families with the cooking ingredients needed to produce the spicy, complex, predominantly vegetarian food they love. Such shops feature an array of fresh vegetables and condiments—green chili peppers, ridged bitter gourd, the tender leaves of fenugreek plants, fresh tamarind pods, tiny eggplants or highly-prized but seasonal mangoes. Shelves are filled with large sacks of rice, many varieties of lentils, containers of ground and whole spices, sticky balls of unrefined sugar and plastic sacks of fresh wheat flatbread (manufactured by a Greek immigrant firm particularly for the Indian, Pakistani, Bangladeshi and Iranian immigrant markets.)

Other shelves hold snack foods, jars of clarified butter, cans of Indian vegetables and fruit and long rows of spicy vegetable pickles in jars. A shopkeeper-importer confides that he sells far more pickles here (many produced in his own Bombay factory) than he ever could in India, because immigrant women in New York lack the time to make their own pickles as they did in India. The grocery's freezer case holds a selection of frozen Indian vegetarian meals newly introduced by an Indian immigrant firm based in New Jersey. Although Indian immigrant women are still a bit shamefaced about using this kind of convenience food, they console themselves with the thought that female relatives in India are also beginning to turn to frozen and prepared food.

The food and spice shops along 74th Street and nearby 37th Avenue testify that the centrality of food and cooking in Indian culture has been carried over into immigrant lives. They also offer insight into the important link between food and Indian immigrant women's self-identification (see also Chapter 5). Like women in India, the first generation of Indian immigrant women tend to see their roles as wives, mothers and caretakers of the family as central to their lives. Gender roles have to some extent shifted with migration; in 1980 Indian immigrant women in the U.S. had a labor force participation rate of 47 percent, close to that of white women (Gardner, Robey and Smith 1985: 27) and far higher than that of women in India. Nevertheless a great many male-female relationships remain traditional within the first immigrant generation; it is a major point of contention with their American-born daughters. Thus the majority of first-generation Indian immigrants remain convinced that, employed or not, women's most important and rewarding social role is as mothers and family caretakers.

As part of this self-image, Indian immigrant women take meal preparation for the family and its guests very seriously. For women cooking and serving meals, especially traditional meals, is both a sign of love and hospitality and a source of their prestige. Women who have gone out to work since moving to the U.S. are reluctant to abandon the time-consuming task of providing Indian meals because it is so closely identified with the nurturing female role. Women in households which remain vegetarian know that their home cooking is better balanced nutritionally than the fast food that lures their children. "Pizza, pizza, pizza, that's all I hear from them," fumed one mother. "It isn't our tradition and it certainly isn't healthy."

Sometimes children rebel against home-cooked Indian food because they see it as a symbol of their difference from non-Indian peers. A 12-year-old Long Island boy's school locker began to smell very bad. When teachers opened it, they found several weeks' worth of home-cooked Indian lunches stashed away. The boy confessed that every day he dumped the lunch his mother had carefully packed for him, then gone off with his friends to buy pizza. This was not, he said tearfully, because he disliked his mother's cooking but because his non-Indian classmates had taunted him mercilessly about eating "that stinky Indian stuff." He begged his teachers not to tell his mother; he knew she would not understand his dilemma, but would be deeply hurt at the rejection of her food.

In families where children's tastes have become Americanized, and where pizzas, potato chips, soft drinks, spaghetti and even hamburgers have infiltrated, mothers nevertheless try to cook "real Indian food" on weekends. Families expect to gather each day for the evening meal, although not everyone necessarily eats at the same time. If there are grandparents in the house, they may eat first in recognition of their higher status. Children also tend to be fed first. Some women still follow the Indian custom, both deferential and hospitable, of serving the meal to others, then eating after everyone else has finished. However many women have embraced a more egalitarian pattern and enjoy sitting down to eat with the whole family.

Since sharing food is also an important part of the socializing and hospitality that Indians love, a big party may engage the women of a family and even some of their neighbors in marathon cooking sessions, as regional and family delicacies are lovingly prepared for large buffet meals. A woman's prestige hinges partly on the number of dishes she can lay before guests. If a hostess can also entertain large numbers of guests at one time, her friends will be even more impressed.

As more and more Indian immigrant women go out to work, this kind of elaborate entertaining becomes difficult to do on a regular basis. Instead the more affluent have begun to meet friends in Indian restaurants or to take the family out to eat for Sunday lunch. The older generation still thinks eating in restaurants is a bit shocking, not very hygienic and a total waste of good money, but younger people are doing more and more of it, just like nonIndian New Yorkers. The practice now appears in urban India as well, where dining out and restaurants for the middle class are far more prevalent than they were fifteen years ago. This shift is just one of the cultural influences which flow back to India from overseas Indian populations.

Many Indian restaurants around New York have become important social centers for Indian immigrant professionals, providing elaborate buffets at lunch and on weekends. These restaurants also compete to cater engagement parties, weddings and Indian organizations' annual events. Other cafeteria-style establishments prepare less expensive, home-style Indian food particularly for working men like taxi drivers, shop clerks or newsstand workers who lack time to go home to eat or have no wives here to cook and pack a meal for them. Indian men do not generally do housework, although a few male students boast of having become expert cooks thanks to advice mailed or telephoned in by their mothers in India.

Sari shops—selling either the graceful, wrapped six-yard garment called a *sari* or the woman's tunic and trousers called *salwar-kameez*, plus yard goods to make men's traditional tunics and coats—are also important in immigrants' efforts to assert ethnic identity and fidelity to Indian culture. Indian immigrant men (except some of the elderly) opt for American-style shirts, trousers and suits for daily wear, as do middle-class men in modern Indian cities. For ceremonial occasions in both India and the U.S. men may wear loose, embroidered, tunic-like shirts or dark, tight-fitting long coats, but the cultural pressure on men to wear traditional dress is less strong than it is on women. Women are the guardians and symbols of tradition in virtually every culture. For women in both India and abroad the cultural symbolism surrounding clothing is emotional and intense; pressures on women to wear "proper Indian clothes" are enormous.

Many Indian immigrant women who grew up wearing saris or salwar-kameez in India continue to dress this way on a daily basis even in the U.S. Tailors working from home make salwar-kameezes and sari blouses to measure (individual fit is important to the overall "look".) The truly fastidious, however, still ask relatives to bring or send garments made to their measure in India by tailors in their old neighborhoods. While some first-generation Indian immigrant women cling to their Indian dress year-round because it is integral to their self-image, others have adopted American clothing for work or school, particularly in the winter. As one woman joked, "I love my saris—I feel most comfortable in them—but the sari looks just awful worn over boots!" Like many women, she opts for trousers and a jacket or loose sweater under her overcoat for trudging to the bus in cold weather. In adopting an American style of dress, she still observes the conventions of Indian modesty which require that a respectable woman keep her legs covered and her bust camouflaged. Her friend, an executive in a large company, wears tailored suits and high heels to the office but changes into Indian clothing when she gets home. Along with their saris or salwar-kameezes many Indian Hindu women wear a *bindi*, a colored dot in the middle of their foreheads, rather as American women wear lipstick. For married women this dot is often red; unmarried women favor black dots, colored dots which match their clothes, or elaborate tear-drop shaped stick-on dots.

Younger, more adventurous women from big Indian cities and second-generation immigrant teenagers usually opt for American clothing all the time. Responding to another kind of cultural pressure, girls favor the international youth uniform of T-shirt, blue jeans and combat boots, perhaps with the addition of a mirrored Indian vest, Indian silk scarf or chunky silver Indian peasant jewelry. Many of these girls eventually cut their hair short, saddening parents and grandparents who still think of long, well-tended hair as a woman's greatest beauty.

Unfortunately some Indian women and girls have given up Indian dress not because they find it impractical or because they want to blend in with American colleagues, but because their Indian clothing or the bindi has made them the target of harassment on the streets. "Wrapped up in a bedsheet" or "Why don't you go home and get dressed—you're walking around in your nightgown" or simply "You're in America now; why can't you wear American clothes?" are some of the humiliating remarks women report having heard directed at them. In some places women have not only been insulted verbally but also shoved and hit on the streets because their Indian dress has identified them as foreign (Chawla 1991). Indian immigrants find malicious attacks against quiet, respectable, modestly-dressed women particularly shocking, reinforcing a feeling that America is more uncouth and uncivilized than they had expected.

Whatever their day-to-day adaptations, virtually all women and girls appear in traditional dress at Indian social events. At concerts, religious ceremonies, or major Indian gatherings the women attending are resplendent in bright colored silk, dainty chiffon, gold or mirrored embroidery. Parents struggle to teach their American-born daughters how to wear Indian dress naturally and gracefully for such occasions. Many Indian organizations sponsor fashion shows, in an effort to convince the young of both sexes that national dress for both men and women is glamorous and fashionable in its own right (Mukhi 1994). Sari shops cater to the tastes of young women by providing salwar-kameez sets with innovative styling; these permit restive young women to feel modern, emancipated and innovative while still wearing "traditional" dress.

The display windows of sari shops along 74th Street show women's clothes in the very latest Indian fashions. This fact suggests a larger cultural phenomenon—the close connection that continues to exist between the New York Indian population and its homeland. The dominant fashion esthetic in clothing still flows from India via Indian fashion and movie magazines and the newest Indian films, alerting New York to what female sophisticates in Delhi or Bombay are wearing. Only the latest prints, the year's fashionable color combinations and the most stylishly-cut kameez or sari bodice will do.

A similar reflection of India's taste is visible in the shops selling music tapes and renting videos of Indian movies. Within weeks of a hit song or popular movie release in India, copies are circulating in New York. For the young, the music on sale may not be traditional Indian music—classical, folk, religious or film music—but forms of pop, rock, disco or rap which fuse Indian and Western genres (see Lipp 1994: B5; Stevenson 1994: A3; Gopinath 1994; Zuberi 1995). Some of this music originates in India but some also comes to New York from the culturally vibrant Indian immigrant populations of Britain, Canada and the Caribbean. Young Indian immigrants like this music because it is a specifically South Asian cultural expression, in tune with their own emerging sense of identity. Certain varieties of this music are also popular because their lyrics contain either expressions of nostalgia for India or messages of social protest.

Since Indians feel women's traditional dress is incomplete without ornate gold jewelry, 74th Street boasts several jewelry stores. The shops' glass cases display a glittering array of 18- and 22-carat jewelry, strings of unset coral and pearls, and ornaments set with semiprecious stones. These expensive items are not simply luxuries for the affluent. The necklaces, earrings, bracelets, rings, hair ornaments, anklets and waist chains on sale are important items in ritual gift-giving. Traditional life cycle ceremonies which are still widely celebrated among the Indian population here require gifts of gold jewelry from family members and close friends. Of course, the fact that immigrants can afford such expensive presents is also a source of pride, a sign that people have succeeded in their new country.

For instance, in immigrant marriages, many still arranged by parents (see Chapter 5), the bride is given a dowry collected by her parents and close relatives. After a young woman's parents have located a suitable groom for her, sometimes with the help of newspaper advertisements or a marriage bureau, an astrologer helps select an auspicious date for the wedding. Parents then begin to assemble their daughter's dowry, for which they may have saved for years. An important component of that dowry is expensive silk saris and gold ornaments.

In the jewelry shops, groups of parents can be seen inspecting jewelry carefully and getting it weighed by the shop clerk, since the price is calculated on the basis of weight. Would this matched set of earrings, necklace, hair ornament and bracelets suit their daughter? Is the design modern enough to please her? Will her new in-laws, who still live in India, approve of it too? Or will they hint that her jewelry is light, cheap stuff given by parents so Americanized that they skimp on a daughter's dowry? Much of a young wife's prestige with her new family hinges on how good her jewels and her saris are, and she will wear her new clothes and jewelry proudly to all parties and events during the first years of her marriage.

In another corner of the shop an elderly couple buys a pair of gold bracelets. They are returning to India for the puberty ceremony of a granddaughter still in India. The bracelets are a gift for the girl, and an advance installment on her dowry. At another counter a young husband contemplates a gold chain for his wife to mark the birth of their first child. "Something simple, please," he tells the young woman shop clerk. His wife has warned him that she cannot wear elaborate Indian-style jewelry to her office. Her American colleagues think it is too flashy. She also worries about attracting chain-snatchers. After all, her best friend had her gold wedding necklace torn off her neck right in the 74th Street subway station at rush hour.

The electronics goods stores in any Little India serve similarly complex social functions while suggesting the mixture of modernity and tradition which characterizes Indians in America. The electronic shops sell the latest gadgets offering, simultaneously, convenience in the home and prestige. Cameras, blenders and food processors, tape decks, cassette players, fine watches and microwave ovens are still expensive and hard-to-get in India. To buy them is a visible sign that the Indian immigrant has succeeded here in the U.S.

The most widely-sold electronic items are color TVs and VCRs, which every immigrant feels are essential household equipment. Sometimes the apartments of those newly-arrived from India contain virtually no furniture other than a TV and VCR. Indians explain that they can wait to buy living-room and dining-room sets, but that without a TV and VCR one is bored, lonely and cut off from the world. Furthermore, most immigrants are convinced that without becoming familiar with American popular culture they cannot become truly American.

Indian families watch many of the same television programs American families enjoy, but they are also devoted to the special Indian programs, broadcast on cable and on Channel 47 particularly on weekends. News programs cover personalities and events within the U.S. Indian population as well as news from India. (Many Indian immigrants remain astounded at how little information American newspapers and network TV news shows carry about India.) Other programs show excerpts and song-and-dance sequences from the latest Indian films and Indian soap operas. Recently some enterprising Indian immigrants have begun to produce local "soaps" which feature Indian immigrant characters beset by the trials, temptations and tragedies of American society.

Additionally, people use their VCRs for one of the most popular forms of family recreation, watching full-length Indian films on video. Most adults prefer these products of India's prolific film industry over American films, which they often find embarrassingly full of bad language, graphic sexuality, violence and cynicism. At one time New York had its own movie house in Manhattan showing new Indian movies, but with the video revolution Indian immigrants, like other Americans, began to stay home to watch rented films. The Bombay Talkies has closed but the video rental shops stocking Indian movies have thrived. Indeed video rental profits keep many struggling small grocery stores afloat.

The other important social function of VCRs is to allow people to participate vicariously—via videotape—in the important events of their widely scattered families. Mr. Charan in Queens showed his guests the full-length video of his brother's wedding in London. Mr. Charan himself could not attend since his struggling small business needs his constant attention to survive, but he did contribute significantly to the cost of the event. Thanks to the video he can admire the looks and jewelry of the bride and derive prestige from the marriage itself. At this gathering Mr. Charan had no need to boast: an expert audience of fellow immigrants watching with him had already mentally calculated the value of the pictured wedding gifts, the cost of the bride's three changes of sari, the expense of feeding all those guests, of hiring four Hindu priests to conduct the ceremony and of renting a horse and convertible car for the various processions to and from the wedding hall.

On another occasion an elderly couple in a big Indian city, too frail to travel, watched a video of their daughter's wedding in a Hindu temple in Chicago, and the American-style reception that followed. They laughed a little sadly: the film showed very clearly that the bride's young women friends had forgotten some of the words to a traditional wedding song. "What's wrong with them?" said the mother as the singers faltered. "They grew up knowing that song. They're losing their culture."

A sharp observer will note that many of the items for sale in the Little India electronics shops require 220 volt current to operate. In other words, these goods are meant for use in India, not in the U.S. These are gift items intended for relatives in India. Present-giving is an integral part of the constant travel to and from India on the part of Indian immigrants and their relatives. Every traveler returning to India must bring back gifts; the longer the absence, the more lavish the presents for all members of the large, extended family, plus some of their long-time servants. Electronic items are prestigious and much in demand, along with Samsonite luggage, fine watches, cameras, blue jeans, nonstick pots and pans, running shoes and sets of unbreakable dinnerware. Gift-giving is a symbol of prestige for both giver and recipient; simultaneously it helps cement a complex set of obligations to kin— obligations which migration and distance have altered but not weakened.

The travel to and from India peaks during December-January and during the summer holiday months of June, July and August. Indian travel agents often book flights for entire families as much as a year in advance; last-minute travellers have to scramble for the few full-price tickets left after all the discounted tickets have been sold. In the warmer months, relatives from India, West Africa, the Middle East Canada or Europe also make return visits to the U.S. Visitors may make a circuit, stopping with a daughter in Philadelphia, a son in Louisiana, cousins in Texas and former neighbors in California. A family's young men are often assigned to what is laughingly called "airport duty," going repeatedly to greet the flights of arriving grandparents, aunts and uncles, cousins and family friends. For dearly-loved or rarely-seen visitors, an entire family welcoming party may be on hand, including babies whom the visitors are meeting for the first time.

Whether returning from a visit to the U.S. or spending one's holiday in India, gifts—electronic items, jewelry, clothing, household utensils and children's toys—are an important part of the travel experience. New York residents planning a trip "back home" often spend weeks shopping. "We can't take back just anything," one New Yorker who was visiting family in India after a five-year absence confided with a small shudder. "They know all the brand names: Nike, Jordache. It will cost us thousands." Still, he did not question his obligation to take back presents for everyone in his extended family.

The flow of items brought to India by visiting immigrants has helped stimulate Indian consumer demand and, in turn, India's own production of items like TV sets, blue jeans or microwave ovens. This is just one of the ways in which out-migration has altered India itself. Nevertheless people in India still love to show off their presents from relatives abroad. "My son brought it. It's made in America. See how good the quality is," they say proudly of something displayed prominently in their homes. The gift is a visible badge of prestige— the prestige of having a close relative who is prospering abroad but has not forgotten family obligations.

Gift-giving allows Indian immigrants to express their continued concern for, and involvement with, their relatives; family members in India reciprocate. Anybody traveling to the U.S. from India not only receives return gifts but is pressed to carry things for friends sending remembrances to their relatives. Homemade pickles, spice mixtures, hard-to-find kitchen utensils, small religious articles, music and religious tapes, video cassettes of family gatherings, packets of photos, clothing and costume jewelry clog the bags of returnees who had hoped to travel light on the way back. These, of course, are simply tokens of affection. More substantially, immigrants' relatives in India loan them investment capital to get a start here, help locate a suitable bride or groom, and help purchase shares on the Indian stock market or urban real estate. Indian immigrants are able to send their sons or daughters back to India for extended holidays or even for several years of education because relatives are willing to house, feed and look after the young people. Thus the flow of gifts in both directions is part of far larger and more sustained exchanges of mutual aid among relatives and friends—mutual aid which is crucial to migration and its success.

3

Creating an Ethnic Infrastructure

CONTINUITY AND ADAPTATION

Equally important in shaping ethnic identity are a series of noncommercial institutions and organizations through which Indians both express and create identity. Among immigrants in New York, some of these institutions and organizations represent cultural continuity, since they attempt to replicate what people knew before migration. Others represent adaptations or innovations, reinterpreting American or New York institutions for immigrants' own purposes. Continuity and change generally coexist in every Indian immigrant event or institution, as elements of traditional culture are reproduced but also adapted and recombined to accord with new American circumstances.

In this chapter I describe a few of the many institutions and annual events which make up what might be called the ethnic infrastructure of the local Indian immigrant population. Ethnic associations, the Ganesha Hindu Temple, cultural societies, major public festivals and the immigrant media supply Indian immigrants with both social and emotional support, helping to ease their accommodation to a new and different society. Additionally it is through these institutions and events that a sense of Indian immigrant identity is preserved, created anew, debated and even fought over.

New York has two long-established organizations which seek to represent the entire Indian immigrant population. The Associations of Indians in America (AIA) is a national organization; local Indians participate in its New York chapter. The Federation of Indian Associations in America (FIA) is a national umbrella group which unifies associations of people from particular regions of India such as Gujaratis, Sindhis, Bengalis, Tamils and Telugus. Both the AIA and FIA perform multiple functions, undertaking lobbying and political representation for Indian immigrants at the national, state and local level as well as helping to organize and sponsor Indian cultural events. Each usually runs an annual conference which entire families are encouraged to attend. These conference discuss issues judged to be of current interest to Indian immigrants.

Despite their aspirations to represent the entire Indian immigrant population, both the AIA and the FIA have greatest relevance to an Indian immigrant elite. Businessmen and professionals, often socially conservative, form their leaderships and shape their activities. Although both associations sponsor some major events which are free, many of their activities, such as dinners, conferences and awards ceremonies, are held in fancy suburban locales and have impressive ticket prices. Many of these occasions are simply too expensive and too inaccessible to interest working-class or lower-middle-class families. People without cars, who cannot afford to pay $50 apiece for entrance tickets, laugh at the notion that they might attend or even get involved with these organizations. "What, me hang around with those rich people? Can't do [it]," scoffed a counterman in a Bronx deli.

Less affluent Indian immigrants are more likely to turn to religious centers or to regional/linguistic associations such as the Sindhi Society or the Gujarati Samaj if they are going to participate in ethnic organizations at all. Many simply retreat into small circles of family and friends, keeping in touch with the larger Indian population only through the immigrant media or through attendance at large, free public events and popular music concerts. A certain number of younger or more liberal Indian immigrants have started their own small organizations which deal with social issues they feel the larger associations have ignored or been too socially conservative to confront (see Chapter 6).

MAINTAINING RELIGIOUS IDENTITY

Religion has been important to every immigrant group making its way in the U.S. over the last century or more. Faith and worship offer support to people who inevitably face periods of great stress, tension and loneliness in the process of relocating and starting new lives. To immigrants, places of worship are not only for prayer or meditation;such places are also social and cultural centers where people meet and talk with fellow immigrants and maintain contact with traditional culture. The music, dance and language lessons which Indian religious centers often offer assist parents trying to instill a sense of cultural identity and ethnic pride in children who never knew India. The Indian immigrant religious institutions also provide certain social services: free meals, donations of used clothing and household utensils, legal advice or free medical screening. At present one Hindu temple has begun to sponsor classes which tutor children for the SAT tests which are so crucial in college entrance, reflecting Indian immigrants' fierce determination to have their children succeed through education.

The population of India is about 80 percent Hindu, and Hindus make up the majority among the Indian immigrants in this country. Thus some of the most numerous Indian religious centers are Hindu temples (Fenton 1988). However, members of India's Muslim, Sikh, Parsi, Christian and Buddhist populations have also settled in the U.S. and some have also established their own religious institutions. Dotted around New York and its suburbs in areas of Indian concentration are a series of Indian Christian churches, Muslim mosques, Sikh *gurdwaras* or Jain or Parsi temples. Some remain small while others have grown into substantial institutions.

In New York most of these religious centers have been created from scratch in the last 25-30 years; the first immigrants, particularly Hindus and Sikhs, found virtually no appropriate religious facilities when they arrived. The first Indian Muslims and Indian Christians to come to New York sometimes shared premises with Muslims or Christians from other ethnic groups. Most quickly sought to find their own spaces, since language and cultural differences usually made the collaboration difficult in spite of common religion.

Often when Indian immigrants first move to an area and are not very numerous, they worship at home. For Hindus in particular this is an acceptable pattern; in New York, as in India, most devout households have a shelf or the corner of a room devoted to prayer, where sacred images and pictures are displayed and incense is burned. However people soon begin to yearn for the sense of community created by public worship (Jha 1995). They miss the familiar large public religious festivals they remember from India, where a yearly cycle of community-wide worship adds color and drama to everyday life.

Furthermore, newly-arrived immigrants are faced with very practical difficulties. How does one name a child, celebrate the arrival of adolescence, get engaged or married, honor a parent's 60th birthday or mark a death in the family in the accustomed manner without religious specialists to perform the proper rituals? To be sure, one can always get married in City Hall, hold an engagement party in a hotel ballroom or seek a funeral home to cremate a dead relative. To make these events emotionally meaningful, however, one needs familiar ceremonies, well-known scripture and the presence of fellow believers.

As the Indian immigrant population grows in an area, people inevitably begin to raise money to establish places of worship and to hire religious specialists to staff them. Groups feel tremendous pride and accomplishment when they eventually raise enough money to rent, buy or build a suitable place and to hire a priest, an imam or minister. Initially when funds are tight the specialist may be a part-timer, a local immigrant trained in ritual and scripture in his youth and now working at some other job. The place of worship may be a drab storefront or the basement of a small house. As congregations grow, however, they are eventually able to hire full-time specialists, often directly from India, for whom the congregation and its religious needs come first.

Likewise, anonymous storefronts and cinder block rooms are gradually enlarged, embellished and transformed into ritual spaces reminiscent of those the immigrants left in India. Hindu temples install images of gods and goddesses imported from India. Sikh gurdwaras need to build cooking facilities, since community kitchens are an important aspect of Sikhism's egalitarian community. Mosques must align their sometimes awkward and inappropriate internal spaces with the direction of Mecca so that worshippers will be able to orient themselves as they pray. Most mosques also eventually have to negotiate the broadcasting of the daily call to prayer with non-Muslim neighbors and community boards.

Many of these mosques, temples, gurdwaras or churches continue to reflect regional traditions within India. People are not content to worship regularly at just any Hindu temple or Muslim mosque; they prefer one which offers the particular kinds of rituals with which they are most familiar. Thus there continue to be a large number of small religious centers around the city catering to people from particular parts of India. At the same time some of these centers are engaged in an effort to become ecumenical, to transcend subcultural differences and to serve the general Indian immigrant population.

THE GANESHA TEMPLE

One of the largest and oldest of the Indian religious institutions in New York City, the Shri Maha Vallabha Ganapati Temple on Bowne Street in Queens, exemplifies the process. Known more familiarly as the Hindu Temple or the Ganesha Temple, the institution was founded in 1977 under the leadership of Indians from southern India. The temple's rituals still reflect South Indian religious practice. At present, however, the temple is engaged in an effort to broaden its appeal to other Hindus. Over the years its congregation has grown, its physical structure continues to be expanded and improved. The daily and yearly cycles of rituals have become more extensive and more elaborate. Today worshippers come to this temple from the entire New York metropolitan area, as well as from the immediate neighborhood. The temple is now also a regular pilgrimage destination for Indian immigrants on holiday in New York from other parts of the U.S. and for visitors from India.

In its earliest incarnation, the temple is said to have been a Polish church, a plain cinder block rectangle with a basement and concrete paving in front and back. Today the temple has been reshaped to look very much like any medium-sized temple in southern India. There is a carved and painted front door, a dome over the roof and a tower decorated with concrete sculptures of gods, goddesses and divine beings. A tall bronze sacred flagstaff was recently installed behind the temple. A big hall for weddings, religious music concerts and large-scale rituals is under construction on an adjacent lot, since temple activities already overflow the basement room now in use. Despite some initial hostility from non-Indian neighbors, the temple continues to expand its area and its activities. (Other newer temples in New Jersey have recently experienced similar hostility.) Furthermore, the Ganesha Temple's presence has now defined one end of Bowne Street as Indian sacred space. The Swaminarayana Temple, constructed by a north Indian Hindu sect from the state of Gjuarat, has been established across the street, while a gurdwara, founded by north Indian Sikhs, operates a block or so away. As one moves down Bowne Street, however, other ethnic territories are visible. A Jewish synagogue is prominent along one block before the street becomes solidly Korean, then Chinese.

The Ganesha Temple is the most inclusive and welcoming of the city's Indian religious centers. An emblem on its facade includes symbols of Hinduism, Islam, Christianity, Judaism and Buddhism, signifying this temple's recognition that all religions seek a common end. Not all Hindu congregations in New York are as ecumenical. For the Ganesha Temple, openness and a welcome to all Hindus and to respectful non-Hindus seems to be a form of adaptation to life in New York, a religious restatement of American multiculturalism.

Inside, the temple has over the years been transformed into an impressive ritual space. At one end of the big room, in the spot of honor, a dark granite image of Ganesh, the elephant-headed god, is installed in a granite shrine. Ganesh, son of the great Indian god Shiva, is the presiding deity of the temple but he is not the only one worshipped here. The walls of the room are lined with other shrines, large and small, dedicated to separate deities. At appropriate times each day priests move from shrine to shrine to say prayers in Sanskrit, make offerings, anoint the images and burn incense.

The statues in the shrines, carved from stone or cast from brass, were made by Indian sculptors especially for this temple. The founding organization, the Hindu Temple Society of North America, is affiliated with the large south Indian temple at Tirupathi, in the Indian state of Andhra Pradesh. The Tirupathi temple donated some of the images, along with some of the funds to establish the temple. Tirupathi's directors also sent the first priests to Bowne Street. As this congregation grew, Tirupathi sent a team of its own sculptors to embellish the building with concrete panels showing scenes from the lives of the gods.

MAINTAINING ORTHODOXY

This active Indian assistance in founding the temple suggests an acute concern among a whole range of Indian religious leaders that Indian immigrants not abandon or dilute their respective faiths, as happened during earlier Indian migrations. For instance, when Indian immigrants were first shipped as indentured sugarcane workers to the Caribbean in the late 1830s, they had few priests in their midst. As desperately poor sugar cane workers, the Caribbean Indian population had little sustained contact with India for many years. As a result, Caribbean forms of Hinduism and Islam have diverged from the forms practiced in India. (Caribbean Hindus in New York have their own separate temples.) Today, India's religious leaders of all denominations are concerned to maintain orthodoxy and standard forms of worship among Indian immigrants abroad.

One way in which faith and religious orthodoxy are promoted is through lecture tours which visiting Indian religious figures make around the U.S. Most of the major denominations arrange such tours. Leaders of religious foundations, saintly, learned men and women, or musicians specializing in a sacred repertoire travel through the U.S. giving sermons (often called "discourses"), concerts and public readings of the scriptures. The touring speakers are often influential in channelling donations from prosperous immigrant worshippers back into religious or charitable projects in India but they also boost religious observance among immigrants here.

This kind of contact with Indian religious figures and Indian religious practice does a great deal to keep immigrants orthodox to Indian practices, while simultaneously reminding worshippers that, although they are a minority in the U.S., they are nevertheless still firmly connected to large religious communities in other parts of the world. In the Indian case migration has often strengthened, rather than weakened, religious orthodoxy, at least for the first generation.

At the Ganesha Temple, morning and early evening bring the largest number of worshippers. At the side door people remove their shoes before entering, as a sign of respect to the deities within. Many bring offerings of fruit, flowers, coconuts or cash, which they hand reverently to one of the priests in attendance. Flowers are woven into garlands which are hung around or above the deities. Coconuts are broken open with a loud crack before being offered at the shrines. Later, when people have finished their prayers, the priest offers each of them a flower from the garland, a piece of coconut, or some ash from the incense, as a token of the god's blessing. As in the secular world, gift exchange is important.

During the busy part of the day, many activities go on simultaneously within the temple. A new bride, nervous and shy in her wedding finery, is circling the shrine to the nine planets in the wake of her new husband, asking a blessing on their marriage. Her mother-in-law supervises the ritual to make sure there are no mistakes which might bring bad luck. In front of another shrine a middle-aged couple is having special prayers said to mark their wedding anniversary. Scattered around the large room groups of people are praying privately before images of favorite deities. Others sit on the thick carpet to meditate or simply to chat quietly with friends. This is perfectly proper; as in India the sacred and the secular mingle easily.

On feast days, when the temple is packed to capacity and it is difficult to see into each shrine, worshippers can watch the rituals on two television monitors hung from the temple ceiling. When no prayers are being offered, the TV sets flash announcements of the temple's forthcoming events and updates on its building program. This kind of technological innovation, like the tiny electric lights which have replaced oil lamps around the shrines or the large digital clock flashing the correct time (so that rituals can begin and end within auspicious time periods) does not strike most Indians as shocking or intrusive. These are simply sensible adaptations of modern technology.

ART AND CULTURE

Downstairs on a weekend the single large room in the temple basement is alive with secular activity. In a side small office off the main room some of the temple's governing body meet to discuss the fund drive; in another side office a temple volunteer sells religious pictures and books. In the main room a group of women lay out a simple vegetarian lunch, free to anyone who wants it. Already several young men, probably students on small budgets, are waiting expectantly. In the middle of the room a group of singers sits on the floor singing *bhajans*, or religious hymns. In India this kind of communal hymn-singing is one of the most popular religious activities. The sweet melodies and simple, catchy refrains praising God make it easy for everyone to join in. As the group in the basement grows in size, many tense, tired-looking singers begin to relax, smile and sway as they sing, immersed in the prayer and the sense of community the song creates.

In one corner of the room a classical dance teacher is organizing her students, six girls from the ages of about 7 to 15 and one little boy. When the hymn singers finish the students will break into beginners' and advanced groups to practice *bharatnatyam* dancing. Unlike the singing, this is an intricate classical dance form which requires years of rigorous study and practice to perfect. Bharatnatyam, with a largely religious repertoire, has been associated with Indian temples for hundreds of years, so it is appropriate that it be taught here. In addition, parents and temple officials see the lessons as part of their overall effort to help Indian immigrant children grasp the basics of Hinduism.

In both India and the U.S., many middle-class young women and a few young men study classical Indian dance, starting as American ballet students do in childhood or early adolescence. New York and New Jersey have a number of Indian classical dance schools taught by distinguished retired dancers. A few of their students will go on to become professionals. Some of the best young American-trained dancers have recently been invited to perform in India, where they have met a certain grudging admiration, even from the highly critical and purist audiences in cities like Madras. Other dancers will abandon their studies when they go to college or get married. They will be left, however, with a lasting appreciation of the art form and of the classical music on which it is based.

One of the advantages for Indian immigrants who live in and around New York City is that there are frequent concerts of classical Indian music and dance. Several Indian immigrant cultural organizations, from the venerable Bharatiya Vidhya Bhavan to Indian regional associations like the Tamil Sangam, sponsor concert tours by the best classical musicians and dancers from India, Canada and the U.S. Classical performances may not sell out Madison Square Garden the way Indian popular music concerts do, but respectable crowds still gather to applaud the best-known artists. The presence of enthusiastic and knowledgeable non-Indian audiences in big U.S. cities such as New York and Chicago has helped Indian immigrants in their efforts to promote and preserve Indian classical music and dance here. In smaller towns across the U.S., Indian immigrants' knowledge of the classical tradition is quickly eroded by the weight of American or Indian pop culture.

The location of music and dance lessons in New York's Ganesha Temple has an additional meaning for Indian-American children and their parents. Participation in these classes links second generation immigrant children to the artistic and religious traditions of India. As parents struggle to retain the high culture they see as one of the finest aspects of their heritage and to incorporate that culture into a new Indian-American identity, music and dance lessons help counterbalance the pervasive influence of American popular culture on children. "Our kids learn all the advertising jingles on TV, all rubbish like that," says an aunt who is chaperoning two dance students. "We want them to learn some culture and some spiritual values too."

Conveying Indian spiritual values to American-raised children is often unexpectedly difficult for immigrants. Their own religious instruction as children in India was fairly straightforward, since virtually everyone in a given community was familiar with the same set of beliefs and assumptions. In the U.S., where children are immersed in new and different sets of beliefs at school and through the media, transmitting tradition becomes more difficult. A Hindu priest sighed over the problems he faces teaching children in another temple's Sunday morning religious classes. He recalled a small child being shown around the temple. After inspecting all the deities the child turned to ask him, "But *Panditji* [dear priest], all these gods....Which one of them is the **real** God?" The answer in India would be that all the Hindu gods are different aspects of a single Divine Presence and thus equally real. This makes less sense to children here who have unconsciously absorbed American ideas of monotheism. "We **have** to find new ways of explaining our tradition," said this priest. "It taxes my mind."

The same effort toward cultural preservation leads the Ganesha Temple to organize language classes to teach children an Indian language. With English prevalent even at home, immigrants want their children to be able to communicate with relatives in India. Ideally, they would also like their children to be able to read the literature they themselves grew up with, although only a few children gain reading fluency.

Sometimes the parental assumption that regular exposure to Indian high culture and Indian religion will keep children culturally Indian is rejected by the young. A sulky teenager remarks, "Yeah, I can sing bhajans. I studied *kathak* [another classical dance form]. So what? **That doesn't make me Indi-**

an. I'm an American." Yet large numbers of young Indian-Americans obviously respond positively to this concern about cultural heritage. Many universities across the U.S. now report that their classes in Hindi, Sanskrit, Urdu, Asian religion or Indian history are filled by the sons and daughters of Indian immigrants. The academic classes are often part of young immigrants' ongoing search for ethnic identity. Members of the second Indian immigrant generation typically begin to engage in this search most seriously when they enter college (see Chapter 6).

Other Indian immigrant religious organizations tackle the problem of cultural preservation and creation of ethnic identity among young people not just through the mosque or temple but through adapting the American institution of children's summer camp for their own ends. In addition to canoeing, handicrafts and campfire songs during the summer holidays, camps for Indian immigrant children teach the elements of Hindu or Sikh belief, bhajans, yoga and Indian languages and culture. For families with the money to travel in the summer, these camps may be followed up by tours of India. Tourist agencies in India now use the Indian immigrant press to promote the educational value of family travel to the country's historic sites, nature preserves and great temples.

FESTIVALS AND PUBLIC SPACE

Up to this point this book has dealt with the creation of ethnicity largely in terms of private activities—the things people do at home or among like-minded fellow ethnics. The other face of ethnic identity, however, is a group's creation of a public image and a public presence for itself. Participation in urban festivals—a long tradition in New York City culture— is one of the ways Indian immigrants make themselves visible, define themselves within the city's multiethnic context, and simultaneously stake their claim, as New Yorkers, to the city itself.

These festivals, celebrating events in the Indian religious calendar or events in recent Indian history, have multiple meanings. Some mirror comparable public festivals in India. By staging American variants, Indian immigrants are recreating familiar urban events which in India were often occasions for solidarity across the lines of class and religion. Insofar as the American forms of these festivals attract a wide range of Indian residents, they create, momentarily, a sense of community in an immigrant population that is otherwise divided by geography and class as well as religion.

These festivals are also the public face Indian immigrants turn outward toward the rest of New York City. In them people highlight for outsiders the aspects of their history, culture and ethnic identity they value most. The festivals are also, of course, Indian immigrants' symbolic assertion that they, like other New Yorkers, are part of the city fabric, with the right to take over a piece of urban turf temporarily, to become part of the city's yearly cycle of events. New York Hispanic churches sponsor a January 6 Day of the Kings parade; New York Italians celebrate Catholic saints' days by parading the saint's image and selling sausage; a massive Caribbean Carnival in Brooklyn marks the official end of summer in New York. Indian immigrants now create their own festivals and annual public events to punctuate the year.

THE TEMPLE CAR FESTIVAL

One of the most recent and most religious of these festivals is the Ganesha Temple's car festival, patterned on similar events sponsored annually by temples in India. In late August or early September (the date shifts according to Hinduism's lunar calendar) the temple celebrates Shri Ganesha Chaturthi, the feast of its patron deity, with a procession which takes several hours to pass through the main streets of the surrounding Queens neighborhood. The "car" is a massive wooden two-wheeled cart, carved and painted brightly and decked with garlands of flowers to carry a small replica of the temple's main Ganesha image in procession. Watched over and steadied by the priests, the image is pulled through the streets. A large crowd of the faithful follow on foot. In India these faithful might themselves have pulled the image on its cart. Here, in the interests of traffic regulation and safety, the cart is pulled by a pickup truck which also carries musicians. From the platform carrying the image, priests and their helpers scatter flower petals, rock sugar and scented rose water on the crowd to symbolize the god's blessings. Periodically they also throw off small packages of sweets.

The festival represents a major accomplishment for temple officials, part of their drive to extend temple activities and to make them more orthodox. Organizers are proud that, overcoming all difficulties, they have recreated a festival which is very much like its Indian original. Yet certain details of the event, such as the prominence of women in its management, are not traditional. In India, women outnumber men in daily worship at temples, and in South India women are also active in efforts to consecrate and fund neighborhood shrines and small temples. However the governance of temples and management of their festivals are, as public not domestic activities, in the hands of men. In the U.S. that is slowly changing. In many parts of this country Indian immigrant women are beginning to press for public and official recognition of their efforts on behalf of Hindu temples, as well as asking to be included in temple management. The Ganesha Temple's governing committee, for instance, is now headed by a woman who has been instrumental in moving the temple toward more elaborate, authentically Indian forms of worship. One of the musicians who played the *nagaswaram* [clarinet-like instrument] for the ceremonial procession in 1994 was also a woman—again a role unheard-of in India.

The Ganesha Temple's festival procession is not only a major event but also a well-mannered show of ethnic and religious self-assertion in the neighborhood. When the temple first acquired its wooden car from India and tried to take it in procession, non-Indian neighbors along the residential street protested. Those who had complained about the noise and traffic generated by the street's Indian religious centers fussed even louder at a custom which struck them as bizarre. Today, with the Indian presence well- established in the area, the car festival goes smoothly. It is escorted by police who stop and redirect traffic. Some neighbors still stare in bewilderment but others now nod and wave. A few Americans from Manhattan even join the procession briefly; Indian worshippers smile and make room for them.

Temple officials and their wives lead the procession, followed by a crowd in which men and boys dance and sing. Some of the dancers are able to keep it up for the duration of the procession; others fall back exhausted in the summer heat. Devout elderly people anxious to keep Lord Ganesha in sight at all times walk closest to the cart, their hands resting on it affectionately. Family parties, groups of women, beautifully dressed teenaged girls chaperoned by their mothers, men, often with children riding on their shoulders, walk alongside or just behind the deity. Those in the procession, like the Ganesha Temple's congregation, are a mixture of middle-class and working-class families. Here and there in the crowd, holding tightly to the god's car, can be seen thin elderly women in cheap but tidy saris. These are domestic servants attending this festival on a rare day off. On most days they work long hours for Indian families, caring for small children or elderly people, doing the cooking and cleaning in households where both parents work. For most servants such outings and days off are rarities.

As the procession reaches a main street and passes a row of Indian shops, it halts while wives of shopkeepers come out to make offerings of burning camphor, sweets and money. The musicians mark this with a special flourish. When the procession turns back into Bowne Street and passes first the Sikh gurdwara and then the Swaminarayana Temple, organizers rush about making sure that sweet packages are tossed to members of these other congregations standing to watch. "Make sure they all get some," mutters a temple official rushing up with another box of pre-packaged sweets. The day is one for a sharing of blessings and asserting Indian unity, not for sectarian rivalry.

When the procession finally returns to the temple, a crowd of temple officials and priests are waiting to greet the returning deity. A drummer steps forward to perform a solo, and the crowd dances again. This time some women and girls also join in. There are murmurs of appreciation when an announcement makes it clear that the drummer is a Muslim. In a period marked by bitter hostilities between Hindus and Muslims in India, it is reassuring to recall the ways in which Hindus and Muslims have traditionally cooperated in such religious festivals. Then as the auspicious hour for Ganesh's return to his home approaches, a small bharatnatyam dancer, decked out in bright silk, flowers and ankle bells, steps forward to dance a prayer of greeting to the god before he is carried back to his temple.

Once back inside, the crowd listens as the temple organizing committee's president offers a vote of thanks to volunteers for their special efforts. She also hands out certificates of appreciation, including some for the non-Indian temple caretakers and security guards. As she declares the festival at a close, the crowd streams out to pick up their *prasadam*, or blessed food, from a tent across the street. While most were following the procession, some male and female volunteers were cooking huge vats of special festival delicacies and dishing them out neatly in hundreds of individual styrofoam boxes. Everybody gets a box; some lay claim to several, for family members at home who could not attend. As people head for their cars and the drive home, the tired priests prepare for evening worship in the temple.

DIWALI IN NEW YORK

In contrast, the annual Diwali festival sponsored by the Association of Indians in America (AIA) is far more secular. It is more clearly oriented toward an Indian upper-middle class and toward non-Indians. It takes place in October at New York's original port on the tip of Manhattan. Festival organizers chose the South Street Seaport site both for its access to the river, where the festival's all-important fireworks can be shot off, and for its historic character and centrality in New York City. Symbolically this is a statement about the importance of Diwali as a citywide festival, not just an Indian event. A smaller Diwali festival often held on a subsequent weekend in Queens' Little India is a more local, Indians-only celebration.

In India Diwali, sometimes called "the feast of lights," celebrates the harvest, the beginning of a new agricultural year, and the victory of good over evil. Unlike many Indian religious festivals, which are purely regional, this one is celebrated in virtually all parts of India with folk drama, bonfires, fireworks and the decoration of buildings with lighted lamps. Although for Hindus this is a religious festival, in many Indian cities Muslims as well as Hindus turn out to enjoy the public aspects of an event which is as much a civic celebration as a religious festival. In recent years, however, right-wing Hindus in some Indian citieshave given the festival a nasty anti-Muslim edge. So far this kind of bigotry has not yet defaced Diwali in New York.

As organized by volunteers from the AIA, the festival blends aspects of Indian Diwali with aspects of New York City street fairs and ethnic cultural festivals. Although much of the activity is directed at eating and having fun, there is also an educational aspect aimed both at non-Indians and at Indian immigrant children who need instruction in culture and history. Booths and tables offer things for children to do: learn to make flower garlands; draw pictures of Rama slaying the demon; get your hands painted with designs in red henna dye; paint t-shirts; learn about decorative colored chalk floor designs; watch the young elephant (rented for the occasion) parade about in a bright harness. A puppet show, intended for children, draws a large crowd of adults as well to watch the mythical hero Rama defeat the evil usurper.

Still other booths contain exhibits designed to show off Indian folk arts: embroidered woolen shawls, glass bracelets and folk toys are for sale. Stonecutters, fabric printers, embroiderers, wood carvers, folk painters and toymakers, whose visits have been partly sponsored by the Indian government, display their techniques and finished work. Many of the craftspeople are Indian villagers who fervently hope to retire on the proceeds of a few sales to wealthy immigrants or to American collectors.

In many years an Indian wedding is reenacted in a small tent while a commentator explains the ritual's symbolism. The yearly reappearance of this event at Diwali suggests how important marriage is for Indian immigrants' self-image. One year as I watched some Americans stood gazing at the lengthy mock ceremony bemused; a group of Indian-American teenagers giggled and made snide remarks. **They** weren't going to go through all that—maybe **they** wouldn't even get married at all! Indian folk dances and a dance- drama, performed by school children, dominated a stage near the water. In 1995 a few non-Indian performers were invited to appear at the end of the day's entertainment program, among them a Senegalese reggae band. These performances were apparently included to provide entertainment and dance music to Indian-American teenagers who grow restive on a relentless diet of Indian folk and classical music.

In the last few years festival organizers have also permitted various Indian immigrant activist groups to rent tables at the event so that they can pass out leaflets and collect funds for anti-racist groups, feminist groups, drug and alcohol treatment programs and AIDS support groups. Their presence suggests the Indian immigrant leadership's grudging but growing acceptance of socially committed organizations as part of the Indian community.

Eating is a major part of this festival—an enthusiasm which unites Indian and non-Indian New Yorkers, all of whom know street fairs stand or fall on the variety of food they offer. As a result, many of the Indian restaurants and sweet shops in the region erect booths at this festival. These, and a collection of enterprising individuals who sell home-cooked regional dishes, provide a cross-section of India's highly varied regional foods. One year a woman behind a food table explained that she was a Parsi (a small religious minority originally from Bombay) who now lived in New Jersey. There are not very many Parsis in the U.S., she says, but she and two friends brought some typical dishes to the festival. "Not for the money; I don't know if we will even clear our costs. But we wanted to say that Parsi food too was available here."

The culmination of the festival comes as dark falls over the water. As troupes of young folk dancers finish enacting the death of the demon king, the fireworks which symbolize the conquest of evil, the triumph of virtue, the power of light to vanquish darkness, begin. The rockets and fountains erupting over the river are supplied by the Grouches. Fireworks from this local Italian-American family firm, which supplies fireworks for all the city's big public events, certify this as a truly New York occasion.

Because of its emphasis on education, folkloric performances and handicrafts, because of its sponsorship by an organization run by the Indian immigrant elite, and perhaps
because it is held in public space associated with "the Americans," this South Street Seaport Diwali celebration seems to
attract more middle- and upper-middle-class Indians than
members of the working class. Indeed in some years the high
point of the festivities for many wealthy Indians has been an
expensive dinner cruise on a boat which leaves the Seaport
docks after the last burst of fireworks has died down.

A smaller Diwali festival organized later in October by
the merchants of Little India in Queens attracts more working-class people. The main feature of this festival is music
from popular films and *bhangra* music played by live bands.
Bhangra, originally a folk dance form from the North Indian
state of Punjab, has been taken over and commercialized by
young Indians both here and in India. It is now a wildly popular form of party dance music. The 74th Street Diwali celebration usually ends with the street full of dancing young
men as dark falls. Women and most of the girls watch from
the sidelines.

The considerable expenses of both events are met by Indian immigrant businesses, whose sponsorship is carefully
noted in printed programs alongside the names of all the organizers. Businessmen garner free advertising in this way.
More importantly, they get a reputation for being public-spir-
ited and generous. As among all newly arrived immigrant
groups, wealthier people convert their money into prestige
by providing well-publicized benefits for the ethnic group as
a whole. Such festivals as this provide a perfect vehicle for
public beneficence.

THE INDIA DAY PARADE

The business motif is still more prominent at the annual India Day parade. Since 1981 this has occurred on a weekend
in late August to mark India's achievement of independence
and nationhood in 1947. In India the day is also marked by
parades and floats, most spectacularly in the capital of New
Delhi. The New York parade travels down lower Madison

Avenue in Manhattan, from 44th to 23rd Street. The primary organizer is the Federation of Indian Associations in America (FIA). Many of the floats, however, are provided by local Indian businesses, whose names and family members are featured prominently. Other floats are provided by Indian organizations and religious groups. Floats honoring the Indian flag, Mahatma Gandhi, the Gujarati Society or world peace are interspersed with others advertising tourism to India (travel agents) or particular kinds of rice (grocery importers).

In some years community organizations such as the Indian Students Association from a local science high school, or Sakhi for Women, the South Asian women's organization, or Indian regional associations such as the Telegu Association send contingents of marchers, since floats are expensive to rent and decorate. Non-Indian high school marching bands provide the music, which competes with the Indian movie song hits blasting from tape decks on virtually every float. Some years the International Society for Krishna Consciousness (ISKCON) and the followers of Shri Chinmoy, two Hindu religious groups with large numbers of non-Indian members, send floats or contingents of marchers in Indian dress, despite the uneasiness many Indian-born Hindus feel toward both organizations.

In 1994 members of the South Asian Lesbian and Gay Association (SALGA) were refused permission to march. Parade organizers felt that homosexuals were a disgrace to "the Indian community." Some also invoked family values, arguing that official acceptance of SALGA's presence might send the wrong message to the young people watching the parade. When the parade began, however, the women's organization called Sakhi invited SALGA members to march alongside them (Chopra 1994: A8), to the chagrin of parade organizers. Although the presence of SALGA marchers shocked and offended many conservative Indian immigrants, the fact that the organization wanted to be present suggests how the social and political concerns of the second generation are beginning to be heard publicly, and how some of these concerns challenge accepted boundaries of the Indian immigrant "community" (see also Chapter 6). A similar ongoing dispute over the inclusion of lesbian and gay Irish in New York's Saint Patrick's Day parade has been taking place for years. The struggle over the parade and symbolic representation of Indians as an ethnic group escalated and broadened its scope in 1995. Several months before the parade, SALGA was again told it could not march, this time on the grounds that it was a South Asian, not a purely Indian, group. Organizations identified as South Asian had no place in an event celebrating India, said the conservatives. There were months of argument and negotiation, with various prominent Indian immigrants pressed into service as mediators. Nothing was resolved so the banned organizations held a protest demonstration along the parade route. Their signs reminded FIA officials "We are also Indians."

The controversy itself and the kinds of alignments that crystallized around it suggest a generational split as well as a major divergence of opinion about political strategy and ethnic identity. This split, which mirrors parallel divergences within other Asian immigrant groups (see Omatsu 1994: 44-45), is new to Indian immigrants in New York but may become more pronounced in the future. Obviously the definition of what it means to be Indian in New York is still the subject of debate and contestation.

At the park where the India Day parade usually terminates a stage is set up for speeches, music and folk dance performances. On the surrounding sidewalks Indian immigrants sell t-shirts, music tapes, food, religious tracts, posters, ready-made clothing and costume jewelry. Leafleters circulate among the crowd, passing out both advertisements and political manifestos. While the affluent among the participants and spectators retire to feast at Indian restaurants on nearby Lexington Avenue, the less affluent remain outdoors until dark, eating street food and enjoying the presence of so many other Indians.

Unlike the temple car festival or the Diwali festival, the India Day Parade has several overtly political purposes. Initially Indian immigrant leaders pressed for the event because they saw it as a symbolic means of establishing Indians as a visible presence within New York's constellation of ethnic groups. If the India Day parade does not draw as many non-ethnic spectators as the Saint Patrick's Day parade or the Puerto Rican Day parade, it nevertheless draws Indians from all over the greater New York area. A cross-section of the Indian immigrant population in the region is present: Hindus, Muslims, Sikhs, elderly people in elaborate traditional dress, visitors from India, youngsters dressed for disco dancing, wealthy people in expensive silk and modestly dressed families from the working-class towns of New Jersey and Long Island. There are crowds of young, single men hoping to catch the eyes of well-dressed, well-chaperoned young women, student intellectuals looking jaded, teenagers with partly shaved heads and t-shirts announcing "Om" [a Sanskrit word of meditation and prayer] or "South Asian Pride."

In addition to presenting a carefully selected image of the ethnic group to outsiders, the parade also advertises its organizers' influence in the wider world of "the Americans." The mayor of New York City and other city officials either march or join FIA leaders and other Indian-American dignitaries on the reviewing stand to watch the parade pass. The banning of the lesbian/gay group in 1995 thinned the ranks of nonIndian city politicians attending.

For all its familiar trappings of New York City ethnic politics, the India Day parade frequently reflects Indian immigrants' ongoing concern with the politics of India as well. Among other things, parade organizers want their New York efforts around the event recognized back in India. One normally blase young man explained, "After all, this is New York; this isn't some small town. They'll definitely hear about this in India."

Every year the parade Grand Marshall, the most honored guest invited to lead the march, is a well-known public figure from India brought over specially for the event. Often the Grand Marshall is a movie superstar; in 1994 the young Indian who won the Miss Universe contest was selected, and she duly dazzled the crowd. Such guests are chosen for their popularity and their noncontroversial status. However in the 1980s, during a period in which the Sikhs in the Indian state of Punjab were demanding independence from India, a prominent Indian general and war hero, who happened to be a Sikh, was named the Grand Marshall. The invitation was a symbol of the (Indian) national unity which AIA and FIA espouse. It was also a peace offering to New York area Sikhs, whose relationship with local Hindus had been badly strained during the preceding year by the Sikh separatist conflict in India. Despite these efforts, Sikhs seem to have avoided participation in the parade recently, although some turn out to watch the show.

THE IMMIGRANT PRESS—A FORUM FOR DEBATE

The establishment of special immigrant media—newspapers, radio or TV shows—marks an important step in any ethnic group's consolidation and self-awareness. Among Indian immigrants, newspapers are still the most influential form of media (see Gall and Gall 1993:21), although radio and TV shows also play a major role in keeping people informed.

The primacy of newspapers for Indian immigrants is carried over from India where, despite the recent inroads of television and cable, most literate urban Indians are still avid news readers, devouring weekly magazines, English-language dailies as sophisticated as any in the world, satirical or muckraking political publications, scandal sheets and movie and women's magazines. Once here, Indian immigrants turn to the equivalent American publications, reading *The New York Times, Time, The National Enquirer* or *Cosmopolitan*. But to get news about India or about Indian immigrants, people depend heavily on Indian immigrant publications, which consequently wield considerable influence. More than any other media, the Indian immigrant newspapers remain an important forum for discussion and debate in a dispersed, diverse population. Through their pages it is possible to understand some of the controversies and cultural debates going on among immigrants still defining their identity.

In New York there are two Indian weekly newspapers. *India Abroad* is the largest of these, with both the most subscribers and the most advertisers. The paper publishes both on the East and West Coasts and also puts out editions which circulate in Europe and in India itself, suggesting the kind of function the paper plays in linking Indian immigrants in various parts of the world. Some Indians in New York scoff at the paper, feeling it is too conservative, that it repeats uncritically the opinions of the Indian government, and that it is obsessed with reporting Indian immigrant professional success stories. Yet virtually all read it, or its fierce rival, *News India-Times*.

Additionally there are two small Indian immigrant magazines published in New York by younger, more liberal Indians. *Samar* (South Asian Magazine for Action and Reflection) and *Massala* (spice in Hindi) provide commentary, debate and literary analysis. Both reflect the sensibilities and political interests of social activists among the second generation and offer something of a counterpoint to discussions in the "mainstream" Indian immigrant media. These magazines publish, for instance, discussions of racism in the U.S. as well as critiques of right-wing politics in India or articles about Indo-British popular music.

India Abroad and *News India-Times* are the easiest places to find a quick digest of the week's events in India, notices of Indian cultural events in the greater New York area, immigration advice and news about which Indian-American children won prizes and scholarships. There are ads for Indian food ("mailed direct to your home—freshness assured"), astrologers, travel agents with cheap tickets to India, telephone companies' special calling rates to India, job listings, ads for both local real estate ("candy store for sale, $10,000 a week turnover") and property for sale in India ("large house plot in posh South Delhi—24 hour water").

With considerable effort, these papers manage to provide detailed news about India soon after it happens. For instance, when Indian prime minister Indira Gandhi was assassinated in 1985, Indians in the U.S. were deeply upset and frantic for more details than the American media could provide. *India Abroad* borrowed facilities from a small, non-Indian weekly nearby so it could put together a special edition devoted to the killing and its political repercussions. Likewise a recent, hotly contested Indian election, in which the ruling party appeared likely to be ousted, was reported in the paper district by district soon after the results were announced in India.

This enables Indians in New York to keep closely connected to events and opinions in India if they wish. News about the U.S. carried by *India Abroad* tends to focus on U.S. trade policy affecting India, U.S. investment in India and threats to Indian immigration emerging from the American Congress. Other articles feature profiles of Indian immigrants who have been successful in professions and business here, reflecting the economic concerns, class outlook and social aspirations of many U.S. Indian immigrants. This emphasis is also part of an ongoing effort on the part of the Indian immigrant elite to define the entire ethnic group in terms of its most successful members.

Like national papers in India, *India Abroad* carries a large section of marriage advertisements each week, in which the relatives of young men and women seek introductions to potential brides or grooms. Newspaper matrimonial columns allow relatives to widen the search and reach a larger pool of possible marriage candidates. To Americans the custom of arranged marriages which the ads reflect seems exotic and strange. To many Indians, however, marriages arranged by parents make perfect sense, which is why they have continued after immigration, despite a certain resistance from American-born young people. It is striking that, through the pages of *India Abroad* and *News India-Times*, the search for marriage partners now extends to Indian populations all over the U.S. and to Canada, India, Europe, Africa and the Middle East as well. For some people in India, Africa or even Britain, marriage to a U.S. citizen or green card holder offers a way to emigrate (see also Chapter 5).

India Abroad's letter and opinion columns make clear that there is a wide range of opinion among Indian immigrants on everything—from the role of men and women within marriage to the political situation in India to what it means to be Indian in America. The paper is clearly an important forum through which Indian immigrants continue to work out a sense of ethnic identity, but it is equally clear that there is little agreement yet about what that identity is or should be.

One of the constant themes of letter writers is a contrast between India and America. Letters decry the technical backwardness, corruption and inefficiency of India. Immigrants visiting India for the holidays pass on their horror stories about conditions in Indian cities or corruption among public officials. At the same time there are also poignant laments for the loss of India's interpersonal warmth and sense of community, which is contrasted with the coldness, materialism and alienation of America. Another common debate is whether Indian immigrants can or should immerse themselves wholeheartedly in becoming American. Some letter-writers say yes, and urge fellow immigrants to stop pining for India, to stop holding themselves aloof from American culture and to assimilate. Incidents of racial or ethnic hostility against Indians, these writers suggest, arise from an American perception that Indians are here to take what they can get but do not really contribute to the society they live in.

In reply, other letter writers offer another model. It is possible, they argue, to retain certain central Indian values while living in a pluralistic America. While praising Americans' work ethic, technical efficiency and meritocracy, these writers see much of American culture as self-indulgent, violent and emotionally empty. Do we want to become American, they ask, so that we can get divorces, indulge in promiscuous sex and become alienated from our children and parents? Do we want to spend our days drinking beer, driving around in fast cars, listening to rock music and waving guns? The only defense against such a fate, these writers suggest, is a determined retention of Indian culture and Indian values. Inevitably other writers urge a middle course, suggesting various ways of blending Indian and American values in daily life.

These debates, rooted in the very real differences between the two cultures, rage in one form or another within every Indian immigrant family and often within each individual. They all point to the enormous emotional issues involved in migration.

4

Migration and the Development of a Transnational Perspective

A GLOBAL ECONOMY AND A GLOBAL WORK FORCE

Immigration on the scale it is now occurring into the U.S. is not simply caused by a set of individual decisions on the part of particular people who decide to move from one country to another. Rather, the migration of Indians and all the other groups who have travelled abroad to find new homes is also a part of larger social and economic changes going on all over the world. These changes, part of the creation of a single world economy, are sometimes called globalization.

Until recently scholars talked about "push" and "pull" factors in migration, debating whether immigrants were "pushed" out of their native countries by poverty and unbearable social conditions or "pulled" into migration by the economic attractions of a foreign country. Current research sees the impetus to migration as more complex, both for individuals and for entire groups of people. Often push and pull factors operate simultaneously. Within a single nation some people migrate to escape joblessness and poverty while others from the same country, with broader horizons and more choices, see migration as one of several options in building a career and obtaining higher living standards.

It is increasingly clear that there is no single impetus for migration and no single profile of a typical immigrant. Amid the many varieties of migrant and many reasons for relocating, class stratification in the country of origin has a great deal to do with who decides to migrate, the circumstances of departure and the migrant's ultimate destination. Moreover pre-migration class status continues to shape the migrant's career after arrival.

Although contemporary migration involves the movement of people from less developed countries to those with more advanced capitalist development, the process is not simply the movement of poor people to richer countries. As the Indian case makes clear, many of the new immigrants arriving in the U.S. were not poor in the societies they came from. Why, then, did they decide to abandon old lives and create new ones abroad? What created the conditions that led up to thousands of individual decisions to leave?

The answer lies in the way modern capitalist growth shapes migration through a complex interaction of forces and events all around the world. In the so-called developed countries like the U.S., which receive immigration, new industries and new technologies have rapidly created new demands for workers. At the same time countries like India, which send immigrants, have experienced only a partial, uneven economic development, creating worker surpluses as well as unsatisfied aspirations and social tensions. It is the growth of an integrated, global economy that ties together changes in developed and underdeveloped countries, so that both become part of a single system.

Today one often hears that we live in a single "global society," united by a common taste for blue jeans, Coca Cola and television. This image contains a certain truth. There are now international tastes in music, dress and films shared by young people in many countries. But to explain why such a trend is occurring one must first look at underlying economic changes.

Economic globalization occurs as investors—who today are likely to be Japanese or Korean as well as American or

German—move money, production plants, media and advertising around the world wherever markets, labor supplies, tax concessions and profits seem best. Their field of operations is now international, with the result that we wear clothing made from Chinese cotton, sewed in Sri Lanka and imported into the U.S. by Korean entrepreneurs. Similarly, Japanese auto manufacturers produce cars in the U.S., Italian eyeglass manufacturers get lenses ground in India for a European market and American publishers have books and journals printed and bound in Malaysia.

Much of this process, of course, has to do with the fact that wages and production costs are lower outside the highly developed countries; global production is highly profitable. At the same time global production serves new consumer markets which have developed as newly affluent middle classes appear in previously underdeveloped countries like India, South Korea or Malaysia. The result is that hiring, production, advertising, marketing and sales have been internationalized in a great many industries during the last twenty years in a way they never were before.

This has had the effect of internationalizing the lives and outlook of large numbers of people. Wealthy young urbanites in the Indian capital of New Delhi drink Coke, wear blue jeans and watch TV, like their counterparts in Stockholm or Rio de Janeiro. Their tastes have all been shaped by the same Western or Western-influenced advertising and media. New Delhi sophisticates can afford to participate in this international consumption thanks to employment in India's new industries. Their consumption is aided by internationalized production: Japanese investors produce Sony TV sets in Malaysia (where wages are lower than in Japan) and sell them aggressively to India's enormous consumer market; Coca Cola has recently won the right to manufacture Coke in India for distribution throughout South Asia; local Indian entrepreneurs struggle to manufacture blue jeans cheaper than the imitation Levis imported into India from South Korea or Singapore.

These recent trends toward globalization of consumption and production encourage migration in several ways. In so-called underdeveloped countries such as India, pervasive

Western images and influences nudge many members of the urban middle class toward migration to the West. Already familiar with Western popular culture and consumer items, well-off urbanites begin to think that the kind of life style and consumption they want can be found more easily abroad. Furthermore, the skills and contacts they have as members of India's educated, English-speaking middle class put the choice about whether to stay or leave within their reach.

At the same time there is now an international demand for skilled labor, so that young, well-educated migrants can realistically hope to find work abroad. Increasingly, just as investors cross international borders to build plants or invest in stocks, employers and workers also cross national boundaries in an ever more fluid labor market. The changing nature of capitalist expansion creates new demands for skilled labor, particularly in science, computer design, finance, management and medicine. The brilliant young softwear designers, the well-trained geneticists or the financial market whiz kids can be hired from anywhere in the world. In fact, they are increasingly hired from underdeveloped countries where wages are relatively lower. And, as formerly underdeveloped countries have begun to catch up with the West over the last decade, a certain number of these immigrant professionals have re-migrated to work for international firms in their native countries (Dunn 1995: A1, B5.).

It is in this context that the U.S. government's 1965 decision to restructure its immigration procedures can be understood. Through that legislation the U.S. opened its job market to an international work force just at the time when modernization was undermining traditional economies and making middle-class people in places like India receptive to the idea of migration and careers abroad.

Modern media and communications technology are important factors in the creation of the new global society; they too encourage migration. Today cheaper, easier travel and communications mean immigrants can remain in closer touch with their families and friends at home than was possible for immigrants of earlier generations. And the migrants' experiences abroad are quickly communicated back home. In India the wonderful tales of life in foreign countries that flow back—through phone calls, photos, letters, videos or holiday visits—tend to spur further migration. Today in India's working-class city neighborhoods everyone can point out someone who has spent time employed in the Middle East or Malaysia and has sent home enough to build a house, set up a small business or buy land. Most middle-class Indian families now have at least one relative who has migrated to the U.S., Europe or Australia. The consumer items brought back as gifts, the money sent home to relatives, the tales about plentiful work, high salaries, inexpensive cars, good schools and abundant consumer goods fuel a sense of discontent and make the young eager to migrate in their turn.

Not only do such role models fire the imaginations of future migrants, but they also become a source of information for those preparing themselves to leave. People seek out immigrants and their relatives to get advice about the kinds of training which will enhance chances for a job abroad, about how to frame visa applications, which foreign colleges to apply to (and how to meet their entrance requirements) and the strategies to follow to find work once overseas.

Not all the information which flows back to India about life in other countries is accurate, or fully understood. Those who have not yet been abroad often hold exaggerated or romantic notions about life in other societies, in which images from Hollywood films and MTV mix with the carefully-edited accounts of success and happiness immigrants send home to their families. People in India frequently believe that everybody in the U.S. is enormously wealthy, that wonderful jobs are to be had for the asking, and that U.S. society is egalitarian, just and well-regulated. Paradoxically there is also a prevalent notion that all Americans are heavy drinkers and sexually lax—notions which permit Indians to retain a sense of cultural superiority.

Now that outmigration has been occurring for some time, the presence of large, well-established Indian immigrant populations abroad lessens the anxieties of prospective migrants, who feel confident that life in an alien society will be cushioned by a network of fellow Indians and familiar, Indian-style institutions created by earlier immigrants. Many a young Indian, venturing off to work or study in New York or

London, has reassured anxious parents that he or she will remain healthy, happy and moral by living among fellow countrymen and eating Indian food. Of course the young migrant's own private fantasies about life in the West may be more exotic.

WHAT PROMOTES MIGRATION FROM INDIA?

As a British colony, India has been enmeshed in earlier versions of a global economy for a long time. Because of this India was historically an exporter of migrants long before the current wave of migration to the West. In the nineteenth century India's poverty and its extreme social stratification played a major role. Today uneven development is also a factor. Contemporary India has—at least in cities—lots of industry, high-rise buildings, airlines, telephones, xerox machines, computers, the world's biggest film industry, even nuclear reactors and a space program. The size of its middle class has increased enormously since the 1960s, and this middle class is now consuming avidly, thanks to improved social mobility, higher salaries and newly available consumer goods.

On the other hand, India's development has not kept pace with population growth. Nor has it evened out vast social inequities in a highly stratified society. If some Indians are better off than they were thirty years ago, there are still millions of people without enough to eat, without education, medical care or an extra change of clothing. The fruits of development are tantalizingly within sight, and yet still out of reach for many, leading Indian intellectuals to talk about the way capitalism actually underdevelops poor nations. In India the social strains imposed by widespread poverty interspersed with new affluence undermines the ability of India's professional and entrepreneurial middle-classes to enjoy their newfound prosperity.

One of the most marked results of India's population growth and urban-centered development is a deteriorating quality of life in many parts of the country. As people from villages and small towns flock into big cities, looking for work and for such modern urban amenities as subsidized food rations, schools, medical care, public transportation and movie theaters, the cities have been unable to cope with the influx. The situation has worsened since the mid-1970s, when India decided to pursue modernizing development through foreign investment and to accept development loans from international lending agencies. As a result the government has had to decrease state expenditure in order to repay this foreign debt.

Today in India there is less and less state and municipal funding available to support public amenities, the legal system, or enforcement of city and environmental ordinances. There are perennial shortages of urban housing, water, electricity, public transportation and classroom space. Middle-class families often flee to new suburban housing estates sprawling across former farm land. In these enclaves residents have showers, washing machines, refrigerators, TV sets, even computers and airconditioners, but not always enough water or electricity to operate them. City streets are choked with squatter settlements, roadside shops and mini-factories, so that the increasing number of private cars and motor scooters can scarcely pass. India's once-good public transportation deteriorates from lack of investment. Air pollution and lung disease are on the increase, not only from the horrible traffic jams but also from the destruction of trees, gardens and public parks as speculative builders execute land-grabs to erect office towers and middle-class apartment complexes.

In such an urban environment, interpersonal relations inevitably suffer. A Calcutta intellectual now living in southern India remarked on the loss of "the sweetness of life" in his native city. The kind of leisurely gentleness, courtesy and humor which used to mark Calcutta civic culture and mediate class and religious differences, he said, has been replaced with abruptness, surliness, suspicion and outright hostility. Without its sophisticated, accommodating spirit, he felt Calcutta's well-known crowding and poverty were no longer bearable. Unlike many Indians of his class, this man has managed to relocate to a part of India that still zealously guards its sweetness of life. Many of his contemporaries, however, have moved abroad.

The scarcity visible in urban social life is mirrored in employment conditions. Under British colonialism Indians gained social mobility through higher education. For several generations, however, India has had an oversupply of the educated unemployed—young men with college degrees but no hope of a job. (Young women college graduates, until very recently, disappeared into marriage, so that their lack of employment was little noticed.)

Economic development has not remedied this, since the supply of job seekers still outstrips the supply of jobs which pay a middle-class wage. Only the top-ranked graduates from the most prestigious colleges can hope for the best jobs. Other college-educated young people often must spend years in underpaid starting positions, or must offer enormous bribes for an entry-level position. (On the other hand, many jobs, once landed, offer a guarantee of lifetime employment, and a pension.) Some people never find jobs. In the past such men grew old supported by their extended families, pursuing hobbies, performing volunteer work or simply idling away their time. Today many young college graduates, women as well as men, contemplate migration instead. If they mount a global job search they may be able to start careers and become wage earners, rather than family dependents, by moving abroad where jobs are more plentiful, better-rewarded and more straightforward to obtain.

When young people in India do secure jobs at home, they may find that the intense personalism of Indian life brings caste or religious discrimination, patronage, corruption or simple envy into the workplace. Prejudiced superiors or spiteful colleagues have been known to block people's promotions, deny them access to scientific equipment or scarce research funds and start damaging rumors about their personal lives. A strict age/status hierarchy at work as well as at home makes it difficult for people to complain effectively to their superiors. Because their jobs have been obtained with so much pain and difficulty, they cannot simply quit and go somewhere else as an American might.

Scientifically trained Indian immigrants are particularly eloquent about how migration has made them able to pursue studies and research careers freely abroad and to win recognition on their own merits. Not only are scientific research facilities here better equipped, they note, but hard work, self-discipline and productivity are rewarded without the harrowing scenes of prejudice, backbiting and intrigue they recall in the Indian institutions they left.

It is not surprising that, in an India increasingly marked by scarcity, tension and incipient chaos, there is an eager audience for tales of the West as an orderly, civilized, well-regulated place, where there is more than enough of everything to go around. Many Indian immigrants in the U.S. start any discussion of their own immigration by reminding listeners that "life is hard in India." Indians who go to Singapore, Malaysia, Australia, Europe or the U.S. as tourists come back marvelling at the clean streets, tidy restaurants, disciplined traffic, the honesty and apparent friendliness of shopkeepers and hotel clerks. For many, social order as much as consumer abundance creates a powerful vision of an alternative life to be found outside of India.

Still, even for the most successful migrants there is a certain sorrow and pain in leaving India. For most Indians "the sweetness of life" lies in the intensity of interpersonal relationships. Large, loyal and affectionate families, intense, life-long friendships, traditions of hospitality and generosity, an intellectual climate of passionate debate, a rich, complex religious and artistic culture—all of these offset the rigors of daily life in India. For most immigrants, cultural life, personal ties and dense social networks can never be fully recreated abroad. Many first-generation Indian immigrants go through periods of loneliness and unhappiness, since they find Americans cold and emotionally withdrawn. Although most immigrants would not want to return permanently to India to live, they frequently experience nostalgia and yearning for the world they have lost.

DEPARTURE AND ARRIVAL

How these various factors affect actual people can be seen in the cases of two very different immigrants: Pradip Menon and Rasheed Mohammed. Although the cases show that personal qualities play a role in success, they also point to critical factors such as class status in India—and the importance of education, social networks and sources of accurate information that come with particular class positions.

Pradip Menon is the kind of Indian immigrant whom fellow immigrants most admire and hold up as a shining example. Modest, charming and formidably competent, he has been extremely successful in his own real estate and construction business only 22 years after arriving in New York. He and his wife Priti are active in Indian immigrant organizations, have large numbers of American as well as Indian friends, and seem to move effortlessly through American society, "blending East and West," as they themselves say. His story suggests the role which elite class position in India plays in helping certain migrants make their way quickly and successfully into the U.S. job market and into the upper rungs of the U.S. professional middle class.

Mr. Menon was born in Poona into a wealthy, Westernized family of professionals and civil servants. He recalls growing up in a household of college-educated men and women, where English as well as local languages were spoken and everyone was familiar with Western literature and Western scientific thought. He himself went to a prestigious university where he studied engineering, then to an equally prestigious school of management, where he received an M.B.A. Mr. Menon says of his circle of college friends and classmates, "We all knew we were going to leave... and we all knew what to expect [abroad]."

Mr. Menon's decision to combine training in science and management was a deliberate one, geared toward migration and a career abroad. He had already heard that recently arrived immigrant engineers were experiencing difficulty getting work in the U.S., or were forced to accept relatively humble starting positions. Scientifically trained M.B.A.s from well-known institutions, however, were said to be in great demand.

That realization suggests how sophisticated and up-to-date Mr. Menon's information about overseas employment conditions actually was. Contrast it with the misplaced aspirations of a middle-aged newsstand worker who arrived with an M.S. in physics from a small, not very prestigious Indian university where he had been retained as a lecturer. His friends in his small Indian town had assured him that he would quickly get a scientific or teaching job here with his qualifications. Nobody took into account the man's poor grasp of spoken English or his outdated scientific training. In the U.S. that professional job unfortunately never materialized, and after several years as a laborer on a relative's farm in California and several more years earning $3 an hour in a New York newsstand, he finally abandoned his effort and returned to India with a deep sense of failure.

In contrast Mr. Menon worked for two years as a manager in a joint British-Indian engineering firm as part of his preparation for migration. In that position Mr. Menon acquired job experience which made him more employable once he arrived here. His parents arranged a marriage for him with Priti, a young woman of similar upper-middle-class background who was also interested in living abroad. They were married before he left and arrived in New York in the early 1970s. Mr. Menon immediately got a managerial job in the business loans department of an international bank. Friends from India already worked at the bank and steered him to the job. His wife found a position in an advertising firm. At the bank Mr. Menon was promoted rapidly and eventually became a vice-president. The couple moved from a Manhattan apartment to a large house in an upper-middle-class suburb on Long Island where their two children attend the local public school.

At some point Mr. Menon realized that he would not be promoted any higher at his Manhattan bank. He had hit the "glass ceiling" on further advancement which many Asians report encountering. Although this blow to his ambitions made him angry, Mr. Menon claims this was not an example of racism or prejudice but a flaw in American corporate culture, which continues to erect barriers against outsiders who have not attended "the right" schools or clubs. Nevertheless he was somewhat disillusioned with the U.S. for the first time.

Many Indian professionals have responded to this sort of check on their careers by starting their own businesses. Mr. Menon's response was to return to India as an executive in an

American multinational firm. Mrs. Menon regretted giving up her New York job but looked forward to seeing family and friends again. The fact that Mr. Menon was able to get a job in India so with little difficulty again suggests how impressive his credentials and social networks were. A certain number of Indian professionals who try to find work in India after years in the U.S. are bitterly disappointed. Indian employers tend to be contemptuous of returned migrants whom they suspect of failure abroad. Why else would they want to return? However, Mr. Menon seemed an ideal executive to an American firm which was just opening offices in India and needed his combination of American-style management skills and Indian-style social skills.

Once back in India, Mr. Menon was not as happy as he had expected to be. The job was prestigious, the pay was enormous by Indian standards and the work environment was thoroughly American. Nevertheless the job did not offer the responsibility or autonomy Mr. Menon wanted. Mrs. Menon was frankly miserable. She could not find an interesting job in Bombay and had to be content with helping a friend run a fashion boutique. The wives of her husband's colleagues seemed boringly obsessed with clothes, money, servants and tennis. Some of her own relatives and old friends criticized her sharply for being too restless, independent and outspoken, "too American."

After two years of intense discussion between Mr. and Mrs. Menon, the family moved back to New York, where Mr. Menon formed his own business. He used savings, loans from friends and bank credit to start a firm buying, renovating and reselling Manhattan real estate. He was encouraged and supported in this by colleagues at his former bank, who hold his ability in high esteem and often refer American customers to him. Mrs. Menon got her old job back and in addition acts as her husband's accountant. As the firm slowly establishes itself, Mr. Menon is looking for ways to begin to invest in India as well.

Although Indian immigrant leaders would like both fellow Indians and the larger American society to see Mr. Menon and his successful career path as typical of all Indian immigrants, they are not. Mr. Menon has been exceptionally resourceful and exceptionally successful in negotiating his way through migration, a brief return migration, and the cultural differences he has encountered along the way. Much of what made it possible were his life-long advantages of elite class status.

Other immigrants have had far more modest successes here. Although most have eventually made their way and managed to support their families, they have also been forced into adjustments and compromises they were not prepared for on arrival. In many cases their less elite class backgrounds in India have forced them to enter the U.S. job market at relatively humble levels. Others have been caught in the U.S. economic recession of the 1980s and 1990s, which made jobs harder to get for immigrants and native-born alike, and intensified anti-immigrant prejudice. The stories of less successful Indian immigrants tend to undermine a common view of Indians as exceptional immigrants who have somehow bypassed periods of economic hardship, psychic pain or the shock of adjusting to a new society.

Rasheed Mohammed came to the U.S. in 1981 through an arranged marriage with the sister of a green-card holder. His wife's brother and sister-in-law, both doctors, had migrated to New York in the early 1970s and then sponsored the migration of the husband's unmarried younger sister. Once she reached the U.S. they looked for a husband for her back in India. They calculated, as a number of immigrant families do, that the offer of permanent residence status in the U.S. via marriage to a green card holder would be very attractive to a potential groom. Indeed, they might not need to provide the sister with much dowry; her green card would suffice to make her a good match. A family friend in India located Rasheed in Lucknow and approached his family with the marriage offer.

To the Mohammed family, the U.S. marriage proposal seemed an enormous stroke of good fortune. Firmly lower-middle-class, with horizons which did not stretch much beyond the city, the family was established, conservative, well-respected, but neither wealthy nor cosmopolitan. Rasheed, with an M.A. in history from the local university and a permanent job as a clerk in a local utility company, was the pride of the family, whose other male members were self-employed tailors and factory workers. Aside from Rasheed, only one brother and none of the sisters had finished high school. Like many Indian families, the Mohammeds had concentrated their resources on educating one child, and that child, now with a college education, good English and beautiful manners, was the family hope for prosperity and status mobility.

When the marriage proposal appeared, Rasheed Mohammed was not particularly anxious to marry or to migrate. Still in his twenties, he had just enrolled in a history M. Phil course (a degree intermediate between an M.A. and a Ph.D.), planning to study while retaining his clerical job. However, the marriage proposal was too good to refuse, since it opened up for the family the possibility of migration to the U.S., something otherwise beyond its reach.

According to the marriage broker, the bride's family was very rich, since both her brother and sister-in-law were doctors—and of course in the U.S. all doctors are millionaires. It was even hinted that the in-laws were prepared to enroll Rasheed in a Ph.D. course and to support him while he studied. Because of their class background, Rasheed and his family had neither the sophistication nor the Westernized social networks with which to evaluate these assertions. They assumed that Rasheed could easily enroll in an American university, earn a Ph.D. quickly, get a good job as a teacher and then sponsor the migration of his brothers.

Rasheed's bride Zinaida came to India for the wedding, spent three months living rather uneasily as a member of his joint family and then went back to the U.S. while Rasheed waited for his own visa so he could join her. When he finally got to New York, Rasheed found a difficult, unexpected situation. Zinaida's brother and his wife were indeed doctors, but not millionaires. They had their own practice but most of their patients were poor Medicaid and Medicare recipients, so their incomes were not as high as those of private doctors. They owned a small house in Queens, but after a few weeks it became clear that they expected their new brother-in-law to find his own apartment for his family. They certainly had no intention of sending him to school or supporting him while he studied.

When Rasheed proved unable to find a job on his own, his new in-laws arranged for him to work as an employee in a subway newsstand in which they held a partnership. (It is quite common for Indian immigrant professionals in New York to have, in addition to their jobs, investments in small businesses which are actually operated by employees.) Mr. Mohammed was thus thrust immediately into one of the more exploitative jobs open to Indian immigrant men in New York. Newsstand work, with its very low wages, long hours and difficult working conditions, is profitable for investors but a dead-end for employees, usually men without other job options (Lessinger 1990).

Earning only $5 an hour, Mr. Mohammed rented a small, shabby apartment on the edge of Spanish Harlem for himself and the now-pregnant Zinaida. He then spent the next few years hunting desperately for a better job. His history degree and prior job experience in India failed to impress American employers. The job search was complicated by the fact that Mr. Mohammed was working twelve-hour shifts, six days a week. He was both exhausted and socially isolated, since he had little time to develop helpful social networks or to meet people who might have advised him and helped him make the best of the job skills he did have. His only personal friend was Srinivas, a hospital pharmacist who bought papers at the newsstand every day and gradually became a friend. Zinaida, who had finished a year of college in the U.S., offered to look for work. Rasheed was furious and insulted. Neither his mother nor his sisters had ever worked outside the home, he said, and his wife would destroy family honor by doing so.

Mr. Mohammed finally had a nervous breakdown. Frustration, humiliation and regret for the life he had abandoned in India combined with overwork and social isolation to drive him to the edge. One day he refused to get up and go to work. He refused to eat. When he spoke at all it was to threaten to return to India; Zinaida and the child could follow if they wished, otherwise he would divorce her. Zinaida, with one child and another on the way, was frantic. Her brother and his wife were unsympathetic. In their view Mr. Mohammed was not ambitious or energetic enough to make his way. Zinaida began to baby-sit for a neighbor's child. The neighbor was a Hispanic single mother of whom Rasheed had always spoken badly. Although Rasheed saw the toddler around the house, he did not know (or pretended not to know) that Zinaida was paid for her services.

At this crisis Srinivas and a friend of Zinaida's brother intervened. They got Mr. Mohammed out of bed, took him for long walks, helped him write a resume and got him to apply for a temporary job as a bank teller. Coached for the interview, Mr. Mohammed got the job and was eventually asked to stay on permanently. After two years he was promoted into the bank's foreign currency division, with more responsibility.

Today, with the white collar job he feels is appropriate to his status, Mr. Mohammed is still a driven man. With a modest salary, he realizes that the only way he can earn enough to sponsor the emigration of his brothers, as he had originally dreamed, is through a second job or a small business. Since Srinivas had similar ambitions, they borrowed the capital from established Indian businessmen to open up a street corner news and candy store in a poor residential area of Manhattan. The rent is low because they have no lease; the building will eventually be demolished. However for the moment it is well-located at a bus stop. The shop sells papers, magazines, hot coffee, buttered rolls, candy and gum, batteries and potato chips. The men take turns operating it until 11 at night and on weekends.

To run the store in the daytime, Mr. Mohammed brought a nephew from Lucknow. He helped the boy get a student visa by arranging his application to a New York City college. Mr. Mohammed pays the boy's tuition, buys him books, clothes and subway tokens, feeds and houses him and gives him a small wage—little more than pocket money. Zinaida cooks the boy breakfast and dinner and pores longingly over his college course catalogue. The nephew, who calls himself Joe as part of his determined effort to Americanize himself, looks after the store from 7 A.M. to 5 P.M. then goes off to evening classes in business administration at the nearby college while Mr. Mohammed or Srinivas take over. Unlike Mr. Mohammed, Joe arrived understanding that he was going to have to struggle to make his way. Because he is young and single, Joe still manages to experience his long days and nights as a thrilling adventure full of wonderful American music, American movies and American girls. Like many other Indian students, he expects to find a way to stay in the U.S. after he finishes college.

Zinaida would still like to work or attend college, but is tied down by two small children, the requirement that she feed and look after Joe, and her husband's disapproval. Meanwhile Mr. Mohammed concentrates, rather grimly, on recreating a kinship network around him in New York by sponsoring the migration of relatives. He dreams of opening a hardware store with his brothers.

The temporary emotional collapse that Mr. Mohammed suffered is an extreme form of the shock, desperation and shame experienced by Indian immigrants who don't "make it" here as they had dreamed. There is the shock of realizing that jobs are scarce, even in the U.S., and that not all Indian qualifications are respected by American employers. Without a support network, people may not know how to showcase their skills or sell themselves on the U.S. job market. People like Mr. Mohammed, who have given up permanent jobs in India in order to migrate, are often particularly bitter.

Furthermore, retreat to India is extremely difficult, although some immigrants do eventually give up and go home. People feel tremendous shame at the prospect of going back to India empty-handed, since this will disappoint family and friends. More modest families in India often rely heavily on their immigrant member to give the family access to prestige, remittances or future immigrant visas. Some families have also borrowed to send the immigrant off. Since the mythology about the U.S. as a land of limitless opportunity and quick success is firmly entrenched in India, anyone who returns without money or a flourishing career is judged very harshly indeed. In extreme cases some immigrants have even cut off contact with India rather than face this condemnation.

TRANSNATIONALISM

Today immigrants not only move back and forth between societies but maintain social relationships and networks which cross national borders. Rather than moving out of an old society and into a new one, they participate simultaneously in several social arenas located in several different parts of the world. For immigrants the effect is to draw their new and old societies into a single unit, representing a new kind of immigrant adjustment that has been labelled "transnationalism" (Schiller, Basch and Blanc-Szanton 1992).

Take for instance, the Indian young professional, now living and working in Australia where she moved with her parents fourteen years ago. With a university job in Australia, Dr. Lata Govindarajan nevertheless spends considerable periods of time in India, doing research while living with her grandparents, aunts, uncles and cousins. She is also spending a term on a research fellowship in New York City. She has professional relationships in the U.S. and Canada, where some of her brothers and sisters have settled in pursuit of their own careers. In each location her kinship connections, combined with her superb professional qualifications, help to insert her into the local academic setting. While Dr. Govindarajan is perhaps an extreme example (most transnational Indian immigrants shuttle back and forth primarily between their adopted country and India), her ability to live simultaneously in the different social spheres of India, Australia and the U.S. is a good example of how the most affluent and well-trained transnational migrants operate.

Her case also raises certain theoretical issues. While older immigration studies might simply have seen Dr. Govindarajan as an immigrant who moved from India to Australia, and might have focused on her highly successful assimilation into her new society, contemporary scholarship uses a more global framework to look at her movement between geographically separated social arenas, then asks what factors make this possible. Such studies go on to ponder how an immigrant population's transnationalism alters such older concepts as "ethnic identity" and "ethnic group" when these groups and identities are formed across national and cultural boundaries. Some of the old analytical distinctions begin to blur.

Although virtually all the recent immigrant groups coming to the U.S. use transnational strategies to some degree, Indian immigrants are among the most consistently transnational in their behavior and outlook. The group's general affluence encourages this, allowing Indian immigrants settled here to travel back to India frequently as well as to spend time in other countries where fellow Indians have relocated. Moreover, Indian immigrants' educational levels, professions and business ventures encourage travel and give them a certain influence and standing wherever they go. A highly trained scientist such as Dr. Govindarajan is welcomed in universities all around the English-speaking world. Large-scale investors like Mr. Menon are also welcomed virtually everywhere.

Obviously not all Indians in the U.S. operate at this level. A few seem to have cut themselves off from India permanently and have rejected transnationalism, either through estrangement from Indian society or through poverty. The less affluent U.S. migrants rarely return to India even to visit. People like Mr. Mohammed cannot afford the trip, feel embarrassed not to meet their relatives' high expectations, and have nothing special in the way of capital or professional expertise to contribute in India. Others might be able to afford the trip occasionally but resist going back because they find themselves alienated from Indian social life.

Mrs. Patel, a part-time employee in a small card shop and wife of a laboratory technician, has returned exactly once in the twenty-five years since the couple migrated to New York. That one trip was to arrange her oldest daughter's marriage, for which the family had saved painfully for years. Would she go back to India again? "Never, ever," Mrs. Patel says vehemently. With her parents dead and her brothers migrated to England and the Middle East, even the traditional Mrs. Patel finds the provincial town where she grew up socially stifling. People gossiped snobbishly about her husband's modest job, their rented apartment and their one car. She prefers her own small circle of religious, middle-aged Indian housewives in Queens who gather in each other's houses to read scripture and sing bhajans.

For some Indian immigrants, however, extensive transnationalism is a way of life. They travel to and from India often, spending substantial periods of time there so that they retain or recreate their participation in Indian society. A number of

Indians in the U.S. aspire to run for political office in India. For instance, a Chicago-based Indian immigrant recently won a seat in the state assembly of his home state, Bihar. Over the years he had periodically taken time off from his Chicago real estate business to return to his native city. Using his own savings and funds raised from fellow immigrants in Chicago, he has carried out small development projects in the urban neighborhood where he was born. Local residents, reportedly impressed by both his wealth and his ability to get things done, elected him to a legislative seat as an independent over local candidates from established Indian political parties (Agnihotri 1995:1,61).

This gentleman's electoral success, and the long-term residence in India it implies, are unusual. The more typical Indian immigrant transnational wants the best of both worlds, the ability to live in both societies and to move back and forth at will. Many Indian immigrants in the U.S. find that business ventures in India are a good way to do this. With the active encouragement of the Indian government, which wants to use immigrant skills and immigrant capital to further Indian development, Indians living abroad have begun to invest money accumulated through migration into profit-making projects in India. This can take many forms: investment in the Indian stock market; purchase of urban real estate; the construction of factories or for-profit hospitals and medical centers in India (Lessinger 1992a, 1992b).

Although profit is certainly a driving motive for the Indo-British or Indian-Americans who invest in India, sentiment also plays a role. Some investors are considering retirement in India, and see the business as a way to provide themselves with income, interests and a social niche if they return. Some hope to generate income for ageing parents or jobs for relatives who did not migrate. Others are simply looking for a reason to spend part of each year in an India they love and cannot forget.

Transnational investors are not an entirely new phenomenon in India. Certain long-established Indian trading families have had business investments all around the world for several generations. Members of some of these families have now migrated to the U.S., extending these families' transnational commercial networks still further. Suman Lahari, for example, went to Hong Kong as a teenager to serve his apprenticeship in a family firm there which made textiles and exported them to India, Singapore and the Middle East. In the late 1960s he came to New York to become a textile importer as well as a retailer selling sari fabric to Indian immigrant customers. His initial import business was partially financed by family capital from Hong Kong. With the impending takeover of Hong Kong by China, many Indian firms are moving their capital abroad, poised to leave Hong Kong altogether. Meanwhile Mr. Lahari has invested in a number of small clothing factories in India, Bangladesh and Sri Lanka, all making clothes for export to the West.

Chandra Patel started in New York as a grocery store owner, but quickly moved into the import trade as well. He uses family contacts and kinship networks in India and Africa to buy fine rice, lentils and dried coconut for resale to other Indian groceries around the U.S. Mr. Patel has invested in a family-run food processing plant in his native state and he imports most of its output to the U.S. Professional investors like S. Vadivelu use their scientific skills and contacts acquired in the U.S. to launch themselves into high-tech entrepreneurship in India. Dr. Vadivelu initially came to the U.S. for graduate work in engineering. After graduation he went on to found a factory in New Jersey which makes electrolytic capacitors. Some years ago he also opened two factories in his home state of Andhra Pradesh, making ceramic capacitors for sale to Indian electronics manufacturers. His father and brothers manage both plants on a daily basis. Dr. Vadivelu himself travels back and forth several times a year to check on his factories on both sides of the globe.

Although Indians and other Asians continue to seek entry into the U.S., a certain number are returning home permanently, in response to a depression in the U.S. and an economic boom in Asia. Indians, Koreans and Taiwanese are in the forefront of this trend (Dunn 1995: A1, B5). Some of the returnees are immigrant investors who decide that they can now settle in India with comfort, since they earn good profits and are their own bosses. Others who return are not entrepreneurs but professionals who put their American educations and job skills to work in multinational corporations which are appearing in India in greater numbers as India opens its doors to foreign investment and high tech development. Again, high salaries make it possible for them to live in the style of the Indian elite. Indian immigrants who follow this path say explicitly that they return because they miss India.

Not all Indians are as grateful as the successful Bihar candidate's constituents for the attentions of transnational migrants, whom they call NRIs (nonresident Indians). There is a combination of envy, resentment and unease among many Indians about the kinds of influence NRIs have the potential to wield. Many people in India fear the NRIs' American incomes, enormous when translated into Indian rupees, as well as their overseas contacts, offer them tremendous political influence. Repeated NRI demands for dual citizenship, which would allow them to vote in India although citizens of the U.S. or Britain, are regularly denied. Critics point out angrily that the Indian government, in its rush to attract NRI investors, is providing them with tax relief, cheap land, special electricity supplies and government loans. In the process this special assistance diverts public money that might be better used to assist local residents and promote local entrepreneurs.

There is a bitter taunt making the rounds in India which says that NRI stands for Not Really Indian. NRIs are accused of causing the Westernization of Indian manners and morals and the destruction of traditional culture. Certainly the country's urban middle class is adopting many Western-style habits previously unknown, such as eating out in restaurants or bathing in tubs rather than with water poured from a bucket. A good deal of Indian folk culture is disappearing under the assault of TV. Indian immigrants, however, are simply the scapegoats, blamed personally for the inevitable social changes resulting from the globalization of India's economy and society.

It is important to remember that the transnational flow of people and ideas goes both ways. Obviously Western attitudes, media and consumer goods are penetrating and changing India, although India is certainly not about to become a replica of the U.S. or Western Europe. Nevertheless, many Indians are, without becoming permanent migrants, spending a good deal of time abroad involved in the life of Indian immigrant populations. Indian religious specialists, musicians, artists, social activists and politicians travel abroad regularly, spending part of each year visiting centers of Indian immigration in the U.S., Canada, Britain and Australia. Through immigrant institutions the visitors propagate Indian culture, collect donations for activities in India, solicit investments and raise political support. Funding from immigrants has been crucial, for instance, in making possible the activities of the right-wing political coalition in India which is bidding for control of the central government. It is no accident that Indian national magazines now regularly carry articles on the activities of Indian immigrants abroad. The immigrants are not seen (and do not see themselves) as cut off from Indian society but as international extensions of it.

At the same time, transnationalism has shaped the activities and outlook of Indian immigrants in the U.S. As noted in previous chapters, Indian immigrants in New York maintain a close interest in Indian fashions, Indian movies, Indian music, Indian politics and Indian religious practices. They do so not just for reasons of cultural pride or nostalgia for past lives but because they still feel closely involved with India, seeing it as their own society. For the same reasons immigrants want their children to understand Indian religions, to speak Indian languages and to maintain contact with their Indian relatives. Social and political controversies in India continue to reverberate, and be refought in New York. Although Indian immigrant populations can never recreate "home" in a foreign land, what happens in India continues to affect Indian immigrant life abroad. It is no longer possible to separate them analytically.

One of the results of this phenomenon is that there is considerable discussion among Indian and Indian immigrant intellectuals about the Indian diaspora and "diasporic identity." People are beginning to ponder the relationships between the nine million or more Indian immigrants now living all around the world, and to ask whether they have some kind of common interests or common identity. Additionally, they are debating what kind of ties immigrant populations should have with India. The debate also extends to the responsibilities India itself should take towards its far-flung sons and daughters, some of whom left "home" only a few years ago and some more than three generations ago. Should India take action, for instance, when Indian immigrant populations in Guyana or Fiji or Sri Lanka suffer ethnic persecution in the countries of which they are now citizens?

These questions led a group of Indian immigrant leaders in New York City to organize the First Global Convention of People of Indian Origin in 1989. The event brought together Indian immigrants from Europe, the Middle East, Southeast Asia, Africa, the Caribbean and North America. In a remarkable feat of organizing, several hundred participants attended panels and cultural performances which dealt in various ways with the question of immigrant identity and Indianness.

The conference was about many things, including the Indian government's efforts to win NRI investments and NRIs' efforts to get more direct government help for their profit-making schemes. Yet an underlying theme was a larger question about the existence of some kind of pan-Indian identity. Was it possible to remain Indian outside of India? Did one remain Indian even with the passage of several generations? The general consensus of conference participants was that there was indeed some kind of pan-Indian identity which has survived time and distance throughout the diaspora. Most participants left deeply moved, with a feeling that such an identity did exist at the level of sentiment, and that a common Indian-ness united people from different parts of the Indian diaspora. Several participants were moved to tears or found themselves euphoric at being in the presence of so many long-lost "brothers and sisters."

Significantly, some of those for whom a sense of Indian identity had greatest emotional significance were people from parts of the world—the Caribbean, Fiji, Singapore, the Middle East—where Indian immigrants have been subject to significant discrimination with the development of ethnic nationalism in those countries. For them, a sense of pan-Indian or diasporic Indian identity holds an emotional appeal just as

India itself provides a potential refuge or source of political protection from persecution.

The existence of transnational identity as a major factor in Indian immigrant life shifts and further complicates the question of ethnic identity as raised in previous chapters. In addition to defining an ethnic identity within a single society like the U.S., globalization and increasing transnationalism also force first-generation Indian immigrants to define their identity vis à vis India. Are immigrants who have spent decades abroad still Indians? Many in India are inclined to say "no" and to point to the immigrants' Americanization, their loss of "pure" Indian culture and their abandonment of the motherland. Are the immigrants Americans? Many of them don't wholly feel they are. That ambivalence is, after all, why they have remained so deeply involved in India.

5

Family, Gender Relations and the Second Generation

FAMILY AS BATTLEFIELD

As immigrants reconstitute families in the United States, the arena of life's closest relationships also becomes a place—sometimes a battlefield—in which some of the dilemmas of being an immigrant and of living astride two cultures are played out. Modernity and tradition, Indian versus American culture, theory and practice, all clash and conflict most acutely within the household and kin group. The sensation of being "the in-betweens" is particularly acute for the second generation, the children of immigrants. Of course, their dilemmas are not new, but recur throughout the history of U.S. immigration. Over the years a number of American writers have made the immigrant family their subject. Henry Roth, Kate Simon, Pete Hamill, Maxine Hong Kingston and Amy Tan among others have described with eloquence, love and rage their experiences as Americanized children growing up in immigrant households. Today young South Asian writers are beginning to add to the discussion, and their work is often the best entry-point to the complexities of Indian immigrant family life. Their contributions to such collections as *Making Waves* (Asian Women United of California 1989), *Our Feet*

Walk The Sky (Women of South Asian Descent Collective 1993), *Living in America* (Rustomji-Kerns 1995) or *Arranged Marriage* (Banerjee Divakaruni 1995) represent Indian immigrant additions to the body of Asian-American literature. The thread of similarity running through all these accounts is remarkable, despite the passage of time and wide cultural differences.

The most intensely felt issues within Indian immigrant families in the U.S. have to do with tensions between autonomy and group membership and with questions of age hierarchy, gender and sexuality. Cultural struggles within the family are particularly acute for the second generation, who are now becoming adults and struggling to define their individual identities in relation to their parents. The issues and potential conflicts which arise between Indian immigrant parents and children and between men and women are complicated the intensity of emotion which Indian immigrants feel toward family life.

Another source of tension arises from the fact that parents frequently feel that within their families they must defend India and Indian culture by preventing the corrupting influences of American society from affecting their children. Yet a certain degree of Americanization is inevitable. Children frequently find that their parents pose all questions of right and wrong in terms of Indian versus American culture, as Agarwal notes (1991:59-60). Often that appeal to India as the standard of good behavior makes little sense to children partially socialized in American schools and American communities, under the influence of American media. Resentful children ask each other, "Where do our parents get those weird ideas?"

FAMILY AND HOUSEHOLD IN INDIA

It is useful to begin by describing the structure of households and the construction of family sentiments in India, since these patterns form a backdrop to immigrant family life in the U.S. Some Indian immigrant adults try to replicate Indian family patterns in the U.S. Others realize that life in a new society requires adaptation even within the inner world of the household, although they are frequently unsure of how to go about the adaptation process. Even the most flexible Indian immigrant parents are frequently nostalgic for the Indian family lives they grew up with. For children raised in the U.S., Indian family practices and ideals frequently seem outdated, unreasonable and repressive. Some more thoughtful young people say that they "only began to understand where Mom and Dad were coming from" when they themselves visited Indian relatives as older adolescents and experienced life in Indian households.

Until the early decades of this century, many middle-and upper-middle-class families in India lived in large, multigenerational joint families. Typically an older couple kept their married sons, the sons' wives and children, as well as unmarried sons and daughters, living with them in a single house, pooling income and sharing expenses. In affluent families a joint household might stretch into four generations and support dozens of adults and their children.

Memoirs and reminiscences suggest that such households were often idyllic for growing children, who always had their cousins as playmates and abundant adult attention and affection from parents, aunts, uncles, grandparents and live-in servants. However adults, particularly young women, often found such households stifling and oppressive since all their activities were controlled by older people and male family members. As young people and females they were frequently denied education, the right to step out of the house, or even unrestricted conversation with their husbands. Nevertheless it was difficult for people to break away and set up on their own. Paradoxically, despite its restrictions, the joint family itself was also people's major source of emotional and social security. One's joint family was culturally obliged to provide shelter, care and love, no matter what; many people found it hard to give up the certainty of the family embrace.

The hierarchies of age and gender patterned all roles within the joint family, so that it functioned efficiently despite its strains. Virtually all household decisions were made by the oldest men, assisted by the oldest women. Younger people had little or no say in managing the household or even their own lives. Women who are now elderly recall that it was their grandfathers, sometimes prompted by their grandmothers, not their own parents, who decided how much education they should get or when they should get married. The system was buttressed by strong cultural notions that family needs and family unity outweighed individual needs, that older people were better equipped to deal with the world than younger ones and that men were uniquely suited to the outer world of action and public affairs while women were uniquely suited to an inner world of family, household and emotion.

In such a setting children were trained from infancy to defer to those older than themselves, females were trained to defer to males (and after puberty to avoid direct interaction with them), and both sexes were taught to subordinate their own wishes to those of the larger group. The warmest, most emotionally intimate relationships within the household grew up not between husbands and wives but between mothers and their children, and between siblings and cousins of the same sex and same general age.

In contemporary India such large, complex households are no longer very numerous. Urban housing shortages and the demands of professional jobs which scatter siblings to different parts of India have helped weaken the joint family system. Modern ideas about personal autonomy and women's rights have also played a role. Today most middle-class Indians live in nuclear families centered around a married couple and their children. Nevertheless these households are often larger, and more flexible in composition, than their modern American counterparts. These households are also closely linked to others of siblings, aunts and uncles, as the extended family now spreads out physically but retains much of its interdependence. Some of the old joint family's ideals, emotional patterns and all-encompassing quality persist in today's households.

For instance, in contemporary India, unlike contemporary America, elderly people or unmarried younger ones are actively discouraged from living on their own. Instead they make their homes with married relatives. To live alone is thought shocking, abnormal and emotionally unhealthy. Most Indians firmly believe that solitude makes people lonely, depressed, sickly and unable to eat properly—and in the case of women places them in actual danger from robbery or rape. Thus many middle-class households in contemporary urban India contain, in addition to parents and children, one or more grandparents, an unmarried uncle or aunt, a young cousin or niece. Because Indian families, far more than their American counterparts, spend a good deal of time traveling for the purpose of making family visits and maintaining kinship ties, households may also contain a shifting series of relatives who come to stay for months at a time. Long traditions of family loyalty and mandatory hospitality demand that these visitors be made welcome.

Today there are wide differences between Indian households in terms of modernity and sophistication. Nevertheless, older habits of gender segregation and female deference persist in Indian families, although in less extreme form than in the past. Husbands and wives now communicate a great deal more than they once did, yet there is still a good deal of subtle social distance between men and women. Spouses may not spend much leisure time in each others' company. When guests come to the house to visit, the hostess may invite the women into a bedroom to socialize apart from the men who sit talking in the living room. Dinner parties frequently break down by gender into two conversational circles. In short, many Indians' closest friends are still people of the same sex and age.

More importantly, men and boys still dominate family life, getting a great deal of pampering and special treatment from women and girls. A middle-aged woman I knew in a large Indian city mimicked her husband as he sat at his ease two feet from the water jar and summoned her from the distant courtyard where she was doing laundry so she could serve him a glass of water. Her female audience rocked with laughter in gleeful recognition. However the mimic, like many Indian women, did not voice her resentment directly to her husband. She conformed, then relieved her feelings with satire. Little boys imitate adult male behavior toward women at an early age. When one 8-year-old imperiously ordered his mother, "Put more pickle on my plate **now**", his lordly air replicated his father's and grandfather's behavior toward his mother. The fact that his mother laughingly complied highlights the special indulgence with which so many families still regard their sons. It is only gradually that daughters are beginning to be given the same consideration and the same opportunities as sons.

Although little boys may sometimes get swelled heads, Indian families still encourage the young to defer to their elders. The boy demanding more pickle would not have dared speak so rudely to his father or his grandfather. Adults routinely show respect and deference to their own parents and other elderly people and avoid contradicting or arguing with them. Grown men, for instance, often smoke or drink only outside the house, ashamed to do so in front of their fathers and mothers. Both smoking and drinking are considered "low" and slightly indecent. Like sex, they are not something one can mention to people older than oneself.

These attitudes about hierarchy are inculcated at a young age. Children, although deeply loved and indulgently treated, are even today expected to be obedient and respectful to adults. They must come promptly when called, refer to older relatives only by their age-appropriate kinship terms, do errands cheerfully and not interrupt when older people are talking. (Boys get somewhat more latitude in this respect than girls.) In other words, children are encouraged to imitate adult status behavior as soon as they can understand it. Middle-class families tend to enforce these requirements with scoldings, an occasional slap or ear-pulling and a great deal of mockery, sarcasm and shaming. It is not thought proper to beat children except in rare, very grave circumstances.

In return for their obedience, Indian children participate directly in all family activities. They go everywhere with their parents and are present for ceremonies, family events, parties, discussions and debates. They are encouraged to imitate adult behavior and to take on family responsibilities as soon as they can. For instance children are often expected to assist in the important tasks of greeting visitors, serving them food or a drink and engaging in polite conversation as soon as they can talk and balance cups properly. This participation helps children to feel the security of membership in a large, well-defined kin group at a very early age. By the time they are adolescent, they come to understand that lapses in manners, failure in school or naughtiness will reflect badly on their kin group which will be seen as having failed to train its young properly.

FAMILY AND HOUSEHOLD IN THE U.S.

As this discussion suggests, in many areas of family life, Indian immigrants' experiences and expectations directly conflict with American norms and patterns, particularly in the areas of personal autonomy and egalitarian interpersonal relationships. Although Indian immigrant households may look, from the outside, rather like their American counterparts, the ideas and emotions behind that family life are frequently different. Indian immigrants are often privately rather critical of American life and culture. One of the things they find most upsetting is what they see as a pitifully inadequate American sense of family. Indeed, Indian immigrants often attribute their success in the U.S. to their own close family relationships.

Americans do not, say many Indian immigrants, lavish enough time, attention and affection on their children, nor do they care enough to discipline and correct them. Americans are criticized for their lack of attention and affection toward their elders, since so many older Americans can be seen living alone without younger relatives to help them. Indian immigrants also feel sorry for their American friends and colleagues who live far away from, and rarely see, their siblings, aunts, uncles and cousins. Because divorce is still rare and difficult in India, the American divorce rate seems extraordinarily high to Indian immigrants and is seen as further proof of American moral degeneracy. Indian immigrants (and particularly immigrant men) view American women and girls as sexually lax, wholly beyond male control.

REBUILDING KIN GROUPS

Since most Indians move to the U.S. as individuals, people's first effort is to recreate around them the households and kinship networks that were so central to their lives in India. These networks are doubly important to people who face inevitable tensions and anxieties and who have not yet developed lasting friendships with Americans or roots in American communities. Since most of the primary migrants to the U.S. are men, their first step is either to sponsor the migration of a wife and children waiting in India or, if unmarried, to find a spouse there.

Once a man gets a U.S. residence permit or green card and finds a job here, his family in India will start to arrange his marriage to a woman of suitable age, status and education who is willing to relocate overseas. Finding brides willing to go to America immediately after marriage once took some searching; not every young woman was willing to confront marriage to a stranger, plus life in a foreign country, without the support of family and friends. Today the overwhelming Indian interest in migration and the West means many young women are willing to take the risk and venture abroad if they get a marriage offer from an immigrant. Men settled in the U.S., Western Europe or Australia are considered highly desirable husbands, if only for the fact that they give access to a more comfortable life for the bride and possible migration for her kin. One can only admire the courage of the women who take such a leap into the unknown virtually alone.

Susheela Joshi, a university professor, tells a story illustrating some of the difficulties for the woman who marries and migrates immediately. Her family in Chandigarh married her in the late 1960s to a twenty-six-year-old scientist she met for the first time when he visited India two weeks before the wedding. When she joined her new husband here, she found him to be undemonstrative and interested primarily in his research work, though not unkind. Susheela was twenty, the well-educated daughter of a large, loving family full of affectionate sisters, cousins and aunts. In a small university apartment in New York she was bitterly lonely and also disillusioned. She had dreamed of a husband who would be a romantic soul-mate, not an absent-minded fellow who came home from the laboratory to demand meals and sex, but otherwise paid little attention to her.

At that time there were few other Indians in her neighborhood to whom Susheela could turn for advice and companionship. Only one of her husband's Indian friends was

married, to a young woman even more frightened and disori-
ented than Susheela. She says that she might well have fled
back to her family in India, despite the disgrace of a broken
marriage, if it had not been for an older American couple living in the same apartment complex. They befriended her,
comforted her and gave her advice on how to make her marriage work, as well as practical tips on managing a household
in American style. Eventually they encouraged her to find a
part-time job and to enroll in a Ph.D. program in a local university. Today the Joshis clearly get on well together, have
children and a large circle of mutual friends, but Susheela still
recalls those first two years as "hellish, the most horrible of
my life."

Not all migrant wives have such a cold welcome and
some join husbands with whom they have already developed
an affectionate relationship. Mr. Raman, now a highly successful manufacturer, recounted his early struggles and his
rise from penniless immigrant to millionaire. Mr. Raman
turned to his wife sitting nearby and said with deep emotion,
"Without this lady, I could never have made it. It is she who
has made everything possible." He went on to describe how
lonely, desperate and unhappy he was during the two years
he hunted for a job or a business opening in New York. He
wanted to bring his wife and child to the U.S. but was afraid
he could not support them. When his wife wrote, begging to
join him, he kept putting her off, thinking she and the child
would be happier living with his parents.

Mrs. Raman blushes and looks pleased at this public tes-
timonial, then she explains her own feelings at that time. She
could tell from her husband's letters how miserable he was,
although he tried not to alarm her. She dreamed about him
lying sick and hungry, with nobody to care for him. A spiteful
sister-in-law hinted that he was keeping her in India because
he had fallen prey to a blond American temptress. Mrs.
Raman didn't believe it, of course, but the thought gnawed at
her.

Mr. Raman takes up the story: he finally gave in to his
wife's pleading letters and sent for her. But he warned her
that life would be difficult in a tiny furnished room with bare-
ly enough money for food. He asked her if she was prepared

for more hardship than she had ever known in her comfortable, middle-class life. Mrs. Raman's answer was an unequivocal "Yes, anything, as long as we can all be together." Once in New York, he says, she threw herself heroically into the struggle to make ends meet and never complained. Mr. Raman still recalls her sitting beside him late at night as they assembled belts, ornamental braids and costume jewelry which he then peddled to garment manufacturers. "For that I must always honor her." The kind of husband-wife relationship which Mr. and Mrs. Raman enjoy is extremely traditional, but also deeply affectionate. It may even have been strengthened by the shared difficulties of migration.

Important as spouses and children are to Indian immigrants, most would also like to have their siblings and even their parents with them as well, although the elderly are often reluctant to migrate. If relatives can come here, through family reunification clauses of the immigration law or through their professional qualifications, they frequently settle down nearby, helped to find jobs and housing by their more established relatives. As one couple said, "Of course it is wonderful for us to have a brother and sister-in-law near us. But it's also important for our kids to have their own cousins to play with." Both parents recalled with fondness their childhoods, and the large play groups of siblings and cousins who rushed about their Madras neighborhood together some thirty years ago.

Once established in the U.S., relatives offer each other material help as well as emotional support. Mr. Singh, an engineering teacher in a New Jersey technical college, decided to invest in a motel in Georgia as he neared retirement. Two sisters, a brother and a brother-in-law, living in different parts of the greater New York area, loaned him much of the capital he needed. When the motel proved profitable under the management of a cousin, this informal family corporation reinvested in other motels in the South and later bought and renovated a run-down hotel in San Francisco. These establishments provided employment with living quarters for other relatives and friends who migrated more recently.

Of course the reestablishment of the family in American does not always go smoothly. Sometimes the hosts complain about the lack of consideration or unrealistic expectations on the part of those they sponsor. Mr. Mohan had awaited his younger brother Sanjeev's arrival eagerly, but had endless complaints once Sanjeev arrived. As Mr. Mohan tells it, the younger man was still, two months after arrival, spending his days watching TV, playing video games and consuming endless snacks and cups of tea served (with increasing irritation) by Mrs. Mohan. Sanjeev was behaving as if he were on extended vacation in the ancestral joint family home. He did not search seriously for a job. He drove about in the used car his brother had bought him to facilitate the job search, but soon began to hint that he needed a new car. Eventually, under his wife's prodding, Mr. Mohan had a firm talk with his brother, articulating among other things the American work ethic and the doctrine of individual responsibility. "We have worked very hard for all the nice things we have; you will have to work hard in your turn." Mr. Mohan went on to remind the younger man, "Here in America we each have to do these things for ourselves."

For the many Indian immigrants whose relatives cannot or will not join them here, friendship circles come to function as surrogate kin groups, offering a familial kind of emotional and practical support. In most cities and towns where Indians have settled, there are groups of couples who visit and telephone each other several times a week and whose children grow up playing and hanging out together. New arrivals who are friends or relatives of existing members are added to the group, which provides valuable help in getting settled and getting started.

These informal friendship networks support members through life crises, although the absence of the older generation's guiding hand is often felt. For instance, when a divorced man in his 30s decided to marry an Indian woman he had met here, neither his family nor hers were able to come from India for the wedding. Instead their friends, also in their 30s, arranged the ceremony and the reception, although several confessed that they felt overwhelmed by the responsibility. In such an important and traditional life cycle ritual, the thirty-somethings would have liked an experienced older person to deal with the priest, bully the caterer, purchase the wedding jewelry, guide them through the rituals and generally take charge.

AUTONOMY AND EQUALITY

The kind of personal autonomy that Mr. Mohan preached to his lazy brother is a major point of difference between Indian and American ideas of person and of family. American society stresses the importance of autonomy and self-reliance, and expects children to develop them at an early age. Ironically, this same sense of autonomy absolves many American children of family responsibilities; they are not, for instance, expected to help entertain guests or wait on older people as Indian children are. Although middle-class American families also experience conflict over children's claims to independence, older adolescents are supposed to become sufficiently autonomous of their parents so that they can decide (albeit with parental consultation) such things as where to go to college, what to major in and what kinds of careers to pursue. American parents are worried if young people in their twenties have not yet begun careers and moved out of the household to their own apartments. They speak anxiously about "pushing them out of the nest." The Indian view sees people as more interdependent and more enmeshed in family. Autonomy is looked on as something which develops later in life in response to marriage and parenthood—not something that adolescents and young adults can expect to exercise properly. The young are kept safely within the family nest as along as possible.

Not surprisingly, issues of autonomy are a major source of conflict between Indian immigrant parents and their teenaged children. Young Indian-Americans of high-school and college age compare themselves with their non-Indian classmates, and repeatedly express frustration at their own parents' efforts to restrict their movements, monitor their behavior and make decisions for them. The young are particularly annoyed because many feel that they understand the American cultural context far better than their parents do, yet the parents insist in making all the decisions. The situation is exacerbated when Indian-American adolescents' growing independence draws them into a separate American youth culture, with its own music, dress, codes and debates. This American youth culture is doubly alien to Indian immigrant parents for being American and for being closed to adults. Except among the highly Westernized rich of big Indian cities, this kind of separate teenage cultural sphere is unknown in India. Many Indian immigrant parents feel simultaneously rejected and fearful when they encounter this American phenomenon when children reach adolescence.

A poignant example of such a clash occurred in the Advani family. Mr. Advani explained to a visitor with some emphasis that although his seventeen-year-old son, Jagdish, wanted to attend the University of New Hampshire, Mr. Advani had directed him to apply to a smaller (and less prestigious) college some twenty miles from the family home in suburban Long Island. "No eighteen-year-old boy is old enough to live away from his family," said Mr. Advani. "He needs to be some place nearby where he can live at home, with his family, where he belongs."

Mrs. Advani was also present during this conversation and she looked pained. As is frequently the case in Indian families, the son had confided in his mother and told her what he could not tell his father directly without seeming disrespectful: that his friends thought the University of New Hampshire was a fine place, and they were all planning to go there if they could. He wanted to go too, both to be with his friends and to taste a little independence, as American college students do. This time Mrs. Advani had failed in her efforts to mediate.

Behind this discussion was a longer-term issue about careers. Mr. Advani simply assumed that Jagdish (or J.D. to his friends) would go to work in the family real estate business after graduation. A number of successful Indian immigrant businesses in New York are now operated by fathers and their sons who have training in American management techniques. Jagdish was willing to consider a business career but he was not prepared to spend the next twenty years working under his father's eye. When describing his parents to friends he usually refers to them as "clueless—though Mom's O.K., she tries." If Jagdish thinks his father is old-fashioned and dictatorial, Mr. Advani sees himself as a careful, loving parent, choosing the best course for an adored but inexperienced son. This kind of clash, rooted in age and cultural differences, can strain immigrant family relationships for years and is all the more painful because family affections are so intense.

Implicit in the dilemma outlined above is also the issue of egalitarian versus hierarchical relationships within the family. For Indian immigrant women and girls, the question of egalitarian relationships, particularly those between men and women, is of burning importance. Indian culture and Indian immigrant culture are male dominated. In contrast, American society, although far from gender-equal, does offer women a wider range of roles and choices. A great many Indian immigrant women seize the new opportunities they find here. Their daughters may claim them as a right. Yet neither older nor younger women assert their autonomy without inner anxieties and explosive family conflicts.

WOMEN AND MEN

Relatively few Indian women migrate to the U.S. on their own, pointing to the ways Indian women, even educated middle-class women, are circumscribed in India. Despite a growing number of women in the Indian work force and a strong Indian women's movement, a traditional view of women as vulnerable, weak and potentially wayward prevails there. It is still accepted wisdom (among women as well as men) that a woman must always be protected, moving through life from the protection of her father and brothers to the protection of her husband and ultimately of her sons. A highly-placed woman executive in south India, unmarried at 55, confessed with a grin that she had to have a guardian when she was transferred to an Indian city in which she had no relatives. If she had not been able to produce an 80-year-old married family friend to act as her male guardian, neither her family nor her employers would have let her take the job. Thus most Indian families are fearful of letting their daughters migrate to the U.S. on their own. A few young women from elite families do make their way here as students; their families usually want to arrange marriages for them, either here or in India, as soon as they finish their training. A few successfully evade the reimposition of control and make their own lives here. Most women, however, migrate to follow or join men.

This does not mean that Indian women are passive, spineless creatures. Far from it. However, most Indian women still prefer to exercise their intelligence, wit and competence within the limits of home and family. Generally Indian and Indian immigrant women continue to believe marriage, childrearing and nurturing the family are their most fulfilling social roles. Those who are employed often see their jobs simply as an extension of their efforts for the family. In India women wage earners tend to cluster in "women's jobs," such as teaching, women's and children's medicine, social work, clerical work or, among working-class women, domestic work, construction work or sweated labor in small factories. Today, in large Indian cities, there are a handful of elite women who have refused to marry, who place career first, who live independently of their families. They are considered disreputable, unfeminine and wildly courageous; they face endless social obstacles, and not surprisingly, they are still rare.

Raised with this set of assumptions about gender roles, Indian women migrate to the U.S. primarily in the dependent position of wives whose futures will be largely determined by their husbands' choice of jobs. Once settled into their lives here, many women are surprised at the subtle pressure to get a job. This is contrary to all the expectations they faced in India. The 1990 census shows that about 55% of the Indian-born women aged 16 to 65 who arrived in New York City in the 1980s are currently in the labor force (City University of New York 1995: Table 3). Some of the pressure on women to work comes from the surrounding American society, where so many women from professional families are employed, and being a housewife is considered old-fashioned. Some of the pressure also comes from the strong emphasis in Indian immigrant culture on money, consumption and getting ahead as a measure of status, as well as from the emphasis on providing financial assistance to relatives. A certain number of Indian immigrant women living in American suburban communities are also driven into the work force through sheer boredom, loneliness and isolation. Many women report that their first real contacts with Americans and the inner aspects of American culture came through the jobs they hold.

Younger and highly educated immigrant women tend to seek work eagerly, or to enroll in college courses preparatory to a career. The flexibility of youth, the more interesting jobs their education places within reach, and the support of their husbands all encourage these women to work and to enjoy it. Overall a high proportion of the Indian immigrant women working in New York are concentrated in health-related jobs and in the professions.

Older immigrant wives and those with little education are often fearful and resentful about having to work since the kinds of jobs in retailing, factory work or service jobs they are likely to get bring them little prestige. As one woman working in a small factory told a women's discussion group, "My family taught us that staying at home and looking after the house was a woman's privilege. Here, where things are supposed to be better for us, why should I drag myself out to work every day?" Nevertheless other women participating in the same discussion defended employment, even in low-status jobs, because of the stimulation, independence and self-respect their work gave them. Several had won the right to work in the face of family opposition.

Indian immigrant men have a range of responses to the question of women's employment. Some, particularly the more sophisticated and professional, encourage their wives, become proud of their wives' careers and successes and even offer some help with housework and child care. Several men remarked that their wives had become far more interesting companions and occupied a more equal role in the family now that they had jobs. Other men only grudgingly permit their wives to work; they value the money women bring in but see working wives as a serious challenge to male control over the family. Such husbands get particularly infuriated when a wife brings home subversive, "modern" or feminist ideas derived from discussions with American women. As one man berated his wife, "You've become proud, arrogant, **American!** You've forgotten who you are!" Some men flatly forbid their wives to work, reminding them that home and children will go to ruin without the constant attention of a mother.

Because most first-generation working women have children and are responsible for housework, cooking, and perhaps the care of an elderly parent-in-law, there is a brisk demand among professional Indian immigrant households for Indian babysitters/housekeepers. Most women hired in these positions are old or very young poor women, brought directly from India as servants. With little education and halting English, these women are often badly treated and poorly paid and have few opportunities to change jobs. Lakshmi, an impoverished middle-class widow in her sixties, comes from Ahmedabad and is distantly related to her employers. Nevertheless, she says her life in a wealthy New York suburb is "slavery." After harried mornings spent getting the children fed and off to school, the middle of each day is a blank of boredom. Her employers are at work, the children at school, and her employer's aged mother dozes. If Indian movie videos come into the house, Lakshmi watches each one over and over, since she finds American soap operas incomprehensible. Her evenings and weekends are hectic; she has to be on hand to cook for the household's stream of guests. Her major recreation and contact with other Indians comes when her employers remember to include her in trips to a Hindu temple or to some Indian public festival. Lakshmi dreams of taking her small savings and returning to India, but does not know if she would be permitted to leave. Her employers keep her passport for her.

Immigrant parents show a range of attitudes towards careers for their daughters. Some parents encourage their daughters as well as their sons to do well in school, attend college and prepare for careers. American colleges and professional schools are full of young Indian-American women studying science, medicine, law, management or finance and planning to move into professional careers with high incomes. Other parents send young women a mixed message, apparently more concerned about their daughters' marriage prospects than their careers. Some retain the Indian belief that a woman with too much education will have difficulty getting married.

The Guptas, for instance, who operated a small building renovation company, insisted that both their sons study science and computing in four-year colleges. Neither young man particularly wanted such a career; one yearned to be a rock musician and the other wanted to be a commercial artist. Yet their parents were adamant that science was the only route to status and financial security. They were content to send their only daughter to a two-year community college, however, and to have her study accounting. They then arranged her marriage when she graduated at 20, explaining that if her husband was willing to let her work she could help him in his business.

If the question of male control over adult women is tense, girls and young women of the second generation face difficulties of their own, having to do with role expectations as well as control over their sexuality. The traditional Indian view is that the chastity of unmarried girls and women must be fiercely guarded, the more so because women are, by nature, highly sexual. Sex outside of marriage, or even the rumor of such, can damage a young woman's reputation irreparably and bring deep shame to her whole family. The erotically charged American youth culture frightens Indian immigrant parents deeply, and many do their best to keep their children, and particularly their daughters, away from such danger.

From puberty onward many Indian immigrant girls find their movements and friendships restricted and closely monitored. Dating or even casual contact with boys are frequently forbidden. Girls may be sent to one of the few remaining all-women colleges in an effort to preserve their "purity." Not surprisingly, young Indian-American women feel that these restrictions and the harping on the dangers of sex are irksome and insulting; many say they feel shamed in front of teachers and American classmates if they have to avoid mixed-sex activities and decline party invitations. Young women are particularly resentful of a double standard which restricts them far more severely than it does their brothers.

Some parents feel they ought to remove their adolescent girls from the U.S. altogether. A normally calm and urbane professional grew agitated talking about his 12-year-old daughter: "My wife and I are trying to be rational about this. But there are so many dangers for kids now! Date rape, drugs, sex, the diseases.... One little mistake can have such terrible, life-long consequences. We are seriously discussing whether we should all move back to India, or at least send our girl to live with my parents." His remarks suggest the way in which traditional Indian preoccupations with keeping girls chaste merge with the contemporary fears about crime, drugs, premarital pregnancy and AIDS shared by American parents of every ethnic group. His view of India as a refuge from the horrors of American society is widely shared. A certain number of parents actually do send their teenagers back to India for varying periods of time during adolescence.

Some Indian immigrant parents are genuinely liberal, trying to adapt American standards of youthful behavior to the Indian immigrant situation in an effort to blend the two cultures. Mr. Menon and his wife explain that they trust their children and feel confident that they have been trained in good morals and common sense. Their daughter Maya was permitted to have her 16th birthday party in a disco, without a chaperone. Her guests, both boys and girls, danced together, but had promised not to drink. However, the Menons are apparently far more advanced than many in their circle. At a social gathering where, in typical Indian fashion, both adults and teenagers were present, Maya innocently mentioned her party. Instantly the adults were besieged by teenagers arguing, "See? **Her** parents let her go to a disco! Why can't **we**?" The adults in their turn pounced on Mr. and Mrs. Menon, and grilled them about their daring decision. A mixed-sex party? In a disco? Dancing? No chaperones? How could they be sure there was no drinking? Was Maya not being encouraged to abandon her culture? Some adults present were openly shocked, others simply in awe that the Menons could be so bold and confident.

Sometimes the attempt to control young women is extreme. A girl of fifteen living on Long Island wore skin-tight jeans and form-fitting shirts like her classmates. When her paternal grandfather came to live with the family, he accused her of being a slut and ordered her to dress "decently" in baggy Indian-style clothes. The girl refused to change her dress, since her parents did not object to it. They had decided that their daughter had a right to follow the same fashions her classmates did, that the jeans were a harmless statement of style, and that her behavior was modest even if her clothes were not. Eventually the grandfather gave the girl a severe whipping with his belt to punish her disobedience and disrespect. The frightened and outraged teenager told her teacher, who felt obliged to report the matter to child protection authorities. The entire family was deeply humiliated to find itself embroiled with the police, Family Court and social workers. Even more shameful, the story spread among local Indian families and also became known to non-Indians. The grandfather soon returned to India.

These kinds of explosive situations breed evasion and hypocrisy. A great many young Indian-Americans complain about a lack of communication with their parents and speak wistfully of the honesty they see within the families of their American friends. As one young man said, "You just can't talk to them. Just because you disagree, the content of what you say simply isn't heard." Dating and sex, common elements of life for young Americans, can rarely be mentioned to Indian immigrant parents without reducing them to panic, rage or hysterical tears.

One brisk young woman confesses, "There's a lot of lying going on, particularly for girls once they go to college. They do everything American students do, or worse. If their parents call them late at night and they're not in their dorm rooms, they claim they were in the library.'I had a paper, a test...' But they're off sleeping with their boyfriends or girlfriends." Young people who decide that they are gay or lesbian face even more severe problems since Indians see homosexuality as deviant and shameful. One young man had trouble smothering his laughter when he told his mother he was gay. "Don't tell your father," she begged, "And please don't let the neighbors know." The young man was amused because he was aware that his non-Indian neighbors had seen him with his boyfriend, knew he was gay and seemed not to care. Only his own parents were in blissful ignorance.

These silences and evasions are especially painful for young Indian-Americans because families are genuinely close and affectionate; young people know how deeply and sincerely their parents love them. They are also pained that parents who claim the authority to decide so much about their children's lives are unable to give guidance on crucial questions of personal identity. A handful of courageous Indian immigrant social workers, doctors and psychiatrists try to raise issues of identity and clashing culture for discussion through articles in the immigrant press and speeches at Indian conventions (see for instance Motwani and Barot-Motwani 1989). They are not always heard, since the Indian immigrant population tends to think self- criticism only weakens "the community" in the eyes of "the Americans."

YOUTHFUL MUSIC AND IDENTITY-BLENDING

Young Indian-Americans are as fond of American popular music and dance as their non-Indian contemporaries, but they also cherish certain musical forms which have become part of their identity as Indian-Americans and, additionally, as Indians in the diaspora. Bhangra music and various forms of hybridized bhangra-rap-reggae-club music-hip hop have evolved primarily among South Asian immigrants in Britain. Today these forms—publicized through tapes, music videos, college radio stations and live concerts—have also become wildly popular among young Indian-Americans.

Bhangra, a form of male folk music and dance from the North Indian state of Punjab, was brought to England by Punjabi immigrants and had, by the 1970s, become entrenched among all South Asians in Britain. Along the way bhangra had absorbed strong stylistic influences from Afro-Caribbean and African-American music and added electronic instruments to the traditional drums and singers (Zuberi 1995; Lipp 1994). By the 1980s bhangra was well-established among second generation Indian-Americans as well. New York area concerts by visiting British bhangra stars like Bindu sell out. Local New York bhangra musicians, like the band XLNC, play at dance parties where both young men and young women dance gleefully in a sea of waving arms, engaged in a call-and-response with the musicians.

Although this music is certainly not traditional in form, older Indian immigrants approve of their children's passion for bhangra; parents view it as safe because it is uniquely Indian. Their approval may be encouraged because lyrics of some bhangra songs are nostalgic evocations of an India left behind (Zuberi 1995: 37; Gopinath 1994: 13-15). Additionally, the older generation is delighted that the young people who attend bhangra concerts or dance parties are likely to meet only fellow Indians there, unlike rock or rap concerts. For those who listen and dance to the music, it has become an emblem of Indian ethnic pride (Lipp 1994). The music is furthermore a taste which connects young Indian immigrants in the U.S. with their Indian immigrant contemporaries in Britain, Canada and the Caribbean.

The Indo-British reggae-rap singer Apache Indian (aka Don Raja aka Steven Kapur), has many fans in New York, suggesting the transnational flow of cultural influences. Apache celebrates Indian-ness through a mischievous blending and bending of ethnic and national categories. He dresses in New York "gangsta" style, with baggy jeans, razor-sculptured hair and wrap-around sunglasses while his name evokes Native Americans. Many of his lyrics are sung in Jamaican English to bhangra rhythms. His hit song "Arranged Marriage," celebrating the submissive Indian wife, is not wholly ironic, according to disapproving feminists (Gopinath 1994: 24). Apache, who has performed in India, is about to release a made-in-India special for British television called "Apache Goes Indian." The film's publicity stills show him riding to the Taj Mahal on an elephant. Apache's move into the pop mainstream and his quirky, hybrid Indian-ness are sources of ethnic pride throughout the diaspora. In fact, Apache has at least one Caribbean imitator, the Guyanese chutney singer Apache Waria. This Apache is also developing a following in New York City.

Some of the British musicians whose work sells among Indians in the U.S. have a more overtly political edge to their work. Aki (Haq Newaz) Qureshi, the son of Pakistani immigrants to England, leads a black-Asian rap group called Fun-Da-Mental and sings under the name Propa-Gandhi. Many of his songs attack racism and call for Afro-Caribbean and

Asian unity against racial hostility. Other songs invoke such African-American leaders as Malcolm X and Louis Farrakhan (Stevenson 1994) or speak of a radicalized Islam (Zuberi 1995:38). The British rock group Echobelly is South Asian and feminist. Its first album, "Everybody's Got One," has one song about the nasty names Asian children are called on school playgrounds and another attacking South Asian patriarchy (Zuberi 1995: 39). These more political musicians do not express nostalgia for a lost life in India or Pakistan and their music is not intended to make listeners feel good. They express instead a direct engagement with social problems that affect immigrants, such as racism and sexism.

MARRIAGES—ARRANGED, SEMI-ARRANGED OR LOVE?

The continued Indian immigrant preoccupation with female chastity is partly an effort to keep women subordinated and partly an effort to maintain an important cultural distinction between "us" and "the Americans." It is also closely connected with the system of arranged marriages. Such marriages, the norm in India, still prevail among Indian immigrants, complete with ostentatious receptions and large dowries provided by the bride's family. As Luthra (1989: 343) points out, the phrase "decent marriage" appearing in the matrimonial ads of immigrant newspapers signals a willingness to give or take dowry.

Arranged marriages are the subject of endless discussion among members of the second generation. Agarwal's sampling of prosperous California immigrants indicates that two thirds of the young people she spoke to rejected arranged marriages, at least in principle, and wanted to select their own mates. (1991:50). Not all manage to do so.

Raju, an aspiring writer, is somebody who has definitely rejected a marriage organized by his parents. Feeling the responsibilities of an only son he agreed some years ago to let his parents introduce him to one or two eligible girls. The dinner parties at which the introductions between the two families took place were, according to Raju, "a farce, a nightmare.

Everybody knew what this was for but everyone was pretending this was an ordinary party but silently thinking: 'Fall in love!' I sat there, she sat there, we were paralyzed and couldn't say a word to each other. I told my parents, 'Enough. Stop.'" Raju has since made his own choice, of a non-Indian artist; he and Ellen are not married but live together. His parents still hope this relationship is "just a phase" which Raju will outgrow and that he will eventually marry an Indian. "Well, they also hope I'll outgrow wanting to be a writer." Raju says. "Sorry. No."

Whatever their ideals, not all young people succeed in choosing their own mates. Many submit, if reluctantly, to having parents guide their choices or choose for them. For instance during the summer of Nalini's sophomore year in college, her parents told her that old friends had proposed a marriage between Nalini and their son. Nalini at first protested vigorously. When her parents asked why and suggested she loved somebody else, she insisted she did not. She simply resented the idea of being told whom to marry when. Her parents begged her to at least meet the young man, and promised not to push her if she disliked him. Nalini agreed reluctantly, and traveled with her parents to another state to meet the man, his parents and sister, and to inspect his apartment. Nalini decided that 26-year-old Dipak was handsome, shared her interest in classical Indian music, behaved politely to her parents and seemed kind. She also liked his sister, who lived near him. His apartment was large and modern. Dipak and his parents even promised that they would pay tuition so Nalini could transfer to a nearby college and finish her BA. The two were married at the end of the summer.

A certain number of young people actually view arranged marriages positively, in preference to the possible heartbreak and rejection involved in American-style dating. The Desais had fallen in love and gotten married as students in India. They migrated to the U.S. partly to escape the resulting family uproar and censure of this "love marriage." They were stunned when their own 22-year-old daughter asked their help in finding a husband. The young woman said she was too afraid of the American dating scene, involving pre-marital sex and potential rejection, to take responsibility for getting married. A year later their 24-year-old son asked for similar help in finding a bride.

Arranged marriage stems from a cultural concern with family unity and family cooperation. Indian society considers the background of a potential bride or groom to be just as important as individual personality when the two family circles join through marriage. Furthermore, since most Indians look on marriage as a lifelong commitment and consider divorce a shameful tragedy, it is practical to ask older people in the family to search out, and investigate, potential spouses and their families. Young people are believed to be too befuddled with romantic notions and sexual yearning to choose sensibly.

In a traditional arranged marriage, an all-points bulletin is broadcast through the network of family and friends when young people reach marriageable age, usually after finishing college or in the later years of graduate training. Newspaper advertisements or marriage brokers may be used to broaden the pool of candidates. Traditionally potential spouses were required to be of the same caste, from the same region of India, of the same general socio-economic status and to be moderately good-looking. Young men are still expected to have employment prospects and young women to have families willing to give good dowries. Within these constraints, the young couple's personal compatibility and common interests were considered, but family elders often put other considerations first.

Today marriage advertisements in U.S. immigrant newspapers like *India Abroad* give indications of how the arranged marriage institution is shifting and adapting in the American context. Phrases such as "no bars" in more and more ads show the declining importance of caste, language group or even religion in mate selection if people are otherwise compatible in terms of education and profession. Additionally, matrimonial notices are beginning to stress personality and interests—such as a sense of humor or an interest in physical fitness—alongside the inevitable height, weight, beauty and professional criteria. The greater attention to individual and personal qualities within the framework of arranged marriages seems to be an adaptive response to American life, which isolates married couples and demands that they be more interdependent, while denying them the support of the extended family.

Even the traditional arranged marriage is not devoid of love and romance. Indians assume that young couples of similar background and interests will gradually develop love and respect for each other after marriage, and that these feelings will be solidified by the responsibilities of parenthood and running a household. In India particularly, gender segregation means that husbands and wives do not necessarily have to become each others' closest friends; that role is taken on by other people of the same sex. In practice Indian arranged marriages, although different in emotional construction from American marriages, are neither cold nor loveless and no more unhappy or likely to fail than marriages elsewhere.

A further adaptation of the arranged marriage to modern life is the emergence of what is often called the "semi-arranged" marriage, both in India and in the U.S. For an urban upper middle class (but not for millions of less fortunate Indians) this is intended to retain parental control while accommodating the youthful yearning for romantic love which is fed by both Indian and American media. Many urban Indian professional families have in the last 15 years begun to introduce suitable, pre-screened young men and women who are then allowed a courtship period during which to decide whether they like each other well enough to marry. (See Narayan 1995 for an insider's account of such a match.) This differs from American-style dating in that parents and friends are still involved in the initial screening, the courtship is much shorter, little or no premarital sex is involved, and there is a pragmatic recognition by both parties that the aim of meeting is marriage. In the U.S. the friendship circles of immigrant adults often operate as informal marriage bureaus, bringing suitable young people into contact so that they choose each other with only minor parental manipulation. Of course even in India there have been, for several generations now, brave individuals who chose for themselves and made love marriages in the face of parental opposition and family ostracism. In the U.S. such marriages are more numerous, since they have support from the larger society and American culture. However they make many first generation parents uneasy and some try to arrange marriages when their children are young to cut off the possibility of a love marriage.

Immigration has added a complicating factor to the institution of arranged marriage. Indian parents in the U.S. have the option of seeking brides or grooms from India or from other parts of the Indian diaspora, as well as from the U.S. Marriages with the children of Indian immigrants in Canada or Britain are common. Certain Indian immigrants arrange to marry their children to people in India, largely to reenforce their own ties with family and friends there. It is no longer hard to locate potential spouses in India because of the widespread eagerness to migrate. For the parents of Indian-American women, there is a financial incentive in that grooms may accept the green card that comes with marriage to a legal resident or citizen in lieu of an expensive dowry of cash, jewelry or a house. Nevertheless there is great potential for exploitation in such arrangements. There are a number of tragic tales about "green card marriages" which collapsed after legal U.S. residence was established.

The question of marrying somebody from India versus marrying a fellow immigrant divides second generation men and young women. The women, with their American-bred sense of independence, tend to prefer young men raised, like themselves, in the U.S. They know that men from India will demand a kind of service and subservience they are not prepared to give. Many also complain that Indian men are shy, poorly dressed, awkward and unsure in American social situations. "They're totally uncool." (These complaints cut both ways. Young men in India believe immigrant women "have lost their culture" and make bad wives: too assertive toward men, unable to adjust to the demands of others, poor cooks and probably unchaste.)

For their part some young Indian-American men rather like the idea of having a "real Indian wife" who will be quiet, humble and certifiably "pure" and who will cater to them as their mothers did. An irate young Indian woman in New Jersey, thinking over those she knows, reports, "You have these lovely girls from India, really beautiful and educated, with

PhDs, getting married off to real losers from here! Ugly guys or guys who haven't even finished high school!.... The parents do that because they couldn't find anyone here willing to marry those idiots. The girls do it for the green card. Their lives are ruined."

The one point on which Indian immigrants and their children generally agree is that it is important to marry and have children. Even young women headed for careers want a husband and one or two children as well. In general the second generation is almost as family-minded as the first. It is perhaps a tribute to Indian immigrant parents that so many young people want families of their own, even if the process of getting married is one of the most stressful in young Indian-American lives. Additionally, many of the second generation, having been strenuously taught to value Indian culture, also agree with their parents about the desirability of marrying a fellow Indian. Of course, some of the second generation have rejected traditional patterns by choosing to live with or marry Americans; others have opted for lesbian or gay relationships. Yet it is important to realize that these choices do not necessarily imply a rejection of Indian culture and Indian identity, but rather represent a recognition of a range of personal options American life offers. These are options the first generation rarely had.

BEING OLD IN AMERICA

One other aspect of family life creates anxiety for Indian immigrants: the problem of aged parents. Many Indian immigrants are genuinely anguished about how to care for their elderly parents across geographical and cultural barriers. Mixed with this is an anxiety about who will look after them when they themselves grow old. They are not sure their Americanized children will want to take them in as they have done (or wish to do) for their own parents. They are convinced that they would not adjust culturally to American retirement communities. Many immigrants are seriously considering retirement to India rather than face the prospect of American leisure villages.

In contemporary India, old people, particularly when they are widowed, live with married sons or sometimes with married daughters. Some travel between households, staying first with one child and then with another in rotation. Unless they are very crotchety and difficult personalities, the elderly play an important and welcome role within the household. The extra effort required to make them comfortable is offset by their value as sources of ritual and practical advice and help with household tasks. There is traditionally a special bond between grandparents and grandchildren, and older people spend a great deal of time playing with grandchildren, taking them on outings or telling them stories. Traditional patterns of deference and courtesy favor the old and ensure that middle-class household routines revolve around their needs. If grandfather needs freshly made tea four times a day, then a daughter-in-law, granddaughter or servant has to be on hand to make and serve it. If grandmother needs somebody to rub her arthritic legs, a child must do it. In addition, older people in India have numerous sources of amusement outside the household: chats with neighbors, visits to and from friends, volunteer community service, attendance at sermons and religious gatherings or pilgrimages to shrines. In all these settings age commands a certain respect.

Indian immigrants often ask their elderly parents to come and live with them here, to share the good things of life the immigrants have worked so hard to earn. Worries about parents back in India become particularly urgent when all the siblings have migrated so that parents are alone. Immigrants worry greatly about parents who are growing frail and are in need of medical care. Efforts to get elderly people to settle in the U.S. are not always successful, however. Some older people are adaptable and find they enjoy America. Mrs. Srinivas came to live with her daughter in Long Island, unsure whether she would like the U.S. or would just stay for a visit. Energetic, warm-hearted and intelligent, she has stayed to become the surrogate grandmother and unofficial social worker in her daughter's circle of friends. Mrs. Srinivas has also made American friends at a local craft center where her crocheting skills are in demand. She is particularly adept at connecting people who have problems with those who can help, and in giving useful advice in intergenerational family crises.

Unfortunately the experience of Mr. Aggarwal, a seventy-year-old widower who came to live with his son's family in suburban Westchester, is more typical. In spite of the family's efforts, after six months the older man grew bored and despondent. He said he felt useless in his son's house. The grandchildren spent a great deal of time away from home, involved in sports and school activities. They clearly did not need him. His daughter-in-law tried hard to make him comfortable, cooking special dishes she knew he liked, but she did a lot of volunteer work and was also out of the house for much of the day. His son worked twelve-hour days and was only available on Sundays.

Old Mr. Aggarwal had no friends of his own age to visit here, was unable to drive and was afraid to venture out of the house on foot in cold weather for fear of slipping on the ice. "Besides, where would I go?" he said. "The mall? I bought everything I needed; they just laugh at my accent." He eventually returned to Bombay, where he lives with his sister's married son and daughter-in-law. He refuses to return to the U.S. even for a visit, claiming to be too old now to travel. The Aggarwals send him money for expenses and try to visit him there once a year in the summer holidays. When the older man suffered repeated dizzy spells, Mr. Aggarwal spent a day on the telephone to India, getting his father admitted to the best local hospital. He then rushed to India and spent several days at his father's bedside.

If immigrants worry about their parents, they are also beginning to worry about their own old age. Many of them feel that they do not have many roots in U.S. society aside from their own children. And they are not sure that their own children, raised in an atmosphere of American individualism, will want take them in when they grow too old to cope on their own. They do not doubt their children's love for them, but realize that American life makes it hard to maintain extended families. They also realize that they themselves have, inadvertently, failed to be role models since their own parents do not live with them.

As more and more immigrants approach the age of retirement, the question of whether and how to retire in India arises. Since the Indian immigrant population is still largely in its 40s, 50s and 60s, it is too early to know what will happen when this first generation retires. Some Indian immigrants cannot decide where they want to retire; their indecision is made greater because their transnational lives pull them in both directions. Nila Mary Paul still works as a nurse in a large New York hospital. Over the years she has sent her children to college here but has also sent money home to her brothers and sisters in the Indian state of Kerala. Some of the money has gone to construct a house outside her native city of Cochin. A brother and a married sister live there but Mrs. Paul would be welcome to join them if she retired in India. Some of Mrs. Paul's money has gone to erect a handsome tombstone over the grave of her deceased parents in Kerala. Later, Mrs. Paul began to think she would like an equally fine tomb for herself. Her dilemma is that she does not know where she will be living when she dies. Her children and her husband want to remain in the U.S. She herself is greatly tempted to return to India. At present she has solved the problem by buying grave plots in both Long Island and Kerala.

There are hints in the increasing numbers of apartment advertisements in the Indian and Indian immigrant press that a number of Indian immigrants are considering retirement in India. The ads describe "American-style" apartments and bungalows in large Indian cities. Tiled bathrooms, air conditioning, landscaping, assured water and electric supplies and 24-hour security are promised by developers hoping to lure immigrants accustomed to suburban American housing. Some of these apartments and bungalows are intended for a Western-influenced Indian elite, but their builders clearly hope to tempt Indian immigrants to buy as well. There is a parallel growth of American-style hospitals and health centers, offering cancer and heart disease treatments more sophisticated and high-tech than anything available in the average Indian hospital or nursing home. It is possible that a sizeable number of Indian immigrants will take their American savings and pensions and return to India, as they have long dreamed, wealthy and successful. The modernizing sector of Indian society makes this option easier and more comfortable than it once was. Yet many immigrants may eventually find that they are really more Americanized than they thought, and may decide to stay in the country they have so ambivalently adopted.

6

"Who Am I?": Activism and Identity

THE EMERGENCE OF ACTIVISM

The emergence of activism and social advocacy among Indians in New York is closely connected to the evolution of Indian immigrant identity. Participation in advocacy activities which address Indian and Asian social, political and economic problems is far from universal among Indian immigrants. Nevertheless activists' programs represent important points in identity development for members of the second generation, contributing (sometimes indirectly) to their self-awareness and ethnic consciousness. Chapter 1 discussed the kinds of racial, ethnic, or pan-ethnic identities that develop among Indian immigrants and their children as they find a niche in American society. Activism, particularly as it has involved younger people born and educated here, has provoked new debates about Indian-ness versus Asian or South Asian identity. It has raised questions about race and class and gender identity and how they intersect with cultural identity and ethnic group formation.

Social activism—in the form of groups which address alcoholism and drug abuse, wife battering, anti-Asian violence, homophobia or the economic exploitation of poorer immigrants—engages only a tiny proportion of New York's Indian immigrant population. Nevertheless the activists and their programs are now a more prominent feature of Indian immigrant life than they were ten years ago. Then, an elite Indian immigrant leadership largely shaped the local Indian population's internal discourse and debates as well as its public face. Leaders and opinion-makers acted as if social and economic problems did not exist among Indians—that only morally lax others, "the Americans," suffered racial discrimination, beat their wives, took drugs or had homosexual children—certainly not Indians.

Today activists are challenging some of these unrealistic and self-righteous images and insisting that Indians suffer, just like other ethnic groups. As a long-term Indian woman activist warned a gathering of Asian and non-Asian legal workers, "This 'model minority' stuff just divides us. We have to get over it." Activist organizations, small as they are, are having an impact on how the larger Indian population thinks and acts. One Indian feminist who runs a women's group charted the changed outlook among local Indians by the reception she got at official Indian social events: "I used to be persona non grata....Nobody would talk to me, just ignored me. Now, they recognize me and greet me; they even praise what I'm doing."

The reasons for the relatively new increase in social concerns are complex. With the growth of the New York area's Indian immigrant population, there are now simply more immigrants who experience the pressures and dislocations of immigration and develop various social problems. Although Indians do not experience more problems than other ethnic groups, they are also not immune to difficulties which range from mental distress to legal problems to crises of gender identity. New York is also now home to Indians from a wider range of backgrounds than before, including more would-be activists. The local Indian immigrant population has always been full of ambitious men and women striving to get good jobs, earn money and get ahead, sometimes to the exclusion of other interests. Now New York is also home to well-trained Indian immigrants with different goals, more concerned to work for social change than to earn money. Some of these people grew up in India within a tradition of liberal social thinking, simple living and voluntary community service. Others have retained from their student days the vigorous Indian university campus traditions of feminism, radical social critique and anti-establishment activism.

Perhaps most important, the Indian immigrant second generation is now reaching adulthood, and developing its own broader outlook on the world. As students on American college campuses, many of these young people were influenced by identity politics or by anti-racist, ethnic solidarity, gay pride or feminist groups they encountered. Some have learned organizing skills and collective action techniques as students. Others with training in psychiatry, education, medicine, law or social work now want to use these professional skills for the benefit of fellow immigrants. Their strong Indian cultural identification reinforces their desire to be of service to fellow Indians. As they take up social issues, the younger, American-born activists have found allies among older immigrant activists born in India. Some of the most committed people have worked on more than one cause or issue and have, over the years, moved on to energize one group after another. As a result of the proliferation of groups and activities, some Indian immigrants are questioning the mythology of Indians' seamless, conflict-free adjustment to U.S. society and the notion that they are morally superior to other Americans.

A strong work ethic, intense family ties and puritanical sexual attitudes have not insulated Indian immigrants from society-wide problems like domestic violence, racism, the threat of AIDS and sexism. Additionally, for all their middle-class aspirations, Indians sometimes find themselves specifically targeted as immigrants, as foreigners and as people of color.

Indian immigrant activists play a particular role in helping their compatriots deal with social problems because they, as Indians, understand in detail the difficulties fellow immigrants face, the family structures they live with, the community gossip they fear, as well as the culturally determined reactions of shame and denial when things go wrong. Activists understand the universal Indian wish to hide both family and ethnic group problems and to treat them as intensely private. Because Indian immigrants feel shamed at having their shortcomings discussed among outsiders, pressure from concerned insiders is far more effective in changing attitudes and behaviors than the efforts of well-intentioned non-Indians. The younger activists, at home in American society, are often well-equipped to bridge the cultural gap and to link immigrants with American institutions such as social service agencies, legal bodies, labor unions and advocacy groups. At the same time, activists are often able to form coalitions with other ethnic or national groups which increase their visibility and effectiveness.

Activists are not, of course, typical of Indian immigrants in general. Most Indians living in the New York area are resolute in trying to blend in with their neighbors. They often avoid involvement in American politics or social causes, anxious not to "make waves" or call undue attention to themselves. Indeed Indian immigrant leaders are constantly urging fellow Indians to get *more* involved with U.S. politics, suggesting that if Indian immigrants would just vote, contribute money to candidates or stand for election themselves the entire ethnic group might have more influence and recognition. When Indian immigrants are willing to become politically active, many lean toward conservative candidates and issues. They do so partly because conservative views and politicians are in the ascendence nationally in the 1990s, and partly because their own class backgrounds and outlooks encourage conservatism on social issues.

For instance, many Indian immigrants support policies like restrictions on immigration and current efforts to cut off "unearned" social benefits to the poor. In doing so Indians mirror attitudes current among non-Indian professionals, businessmen and affluent suburbanites about the evils of welfare, the economic drain caused by too many immigrants, the cost of social services and the unreasonable demands of the dependent poor. As established, successful Indians recall their own early struggles to get an education in a poor country, to migrate from India and to make their way here unaided, they tend to share the conservative view that the American-born poor, particularly the minority poor, are pampered and lazy. Indians insist on the value of self-help.

They believe that because they "made it" here on their own, poverty and discrimination are no barriers to anyone who is intelligent and determined.

Indians bring with them from India a series of caste/class prejudices about the innate bad qualities and stupidities of lower caste people and the poor (in India most low caste people are still extremely poor.) These views, which most Indians hold unexamined, dovetail neatly with American race prejudice so that Indian immigrants' general complacency often takes a racist twist. It remains to be seen how Indians will respond to current legislative efforts to restrict immigration (Holmes 1995) since the legislation will directly affect Indian immigrants' ability to sponsor the migration of relatives and get them professional jobs.

Indian immigrant intellectual Dinesh D'Souza, currently prominent for his promotion of an ultra-conservative social agenda, upholds an extreme form of these views. D'Souza insists that affirmative action is unnecessary because racism is simply no longer a problem in the U.S. He regards African-American culture as inferior and damaging to mainstream American society. To justify his positions, D'Souza has invoked his own immigrant background. He implies that if he, an immigrant of color, has managed to prosper here, there should be no impediment to African-Americans doing equally well. If they have failed and remain outside of America's social and economic mainstream, it must be their own fault.

D'Souza's position, widely condemned for its blatant racism (Lewis 1995: A 33), is fortunately not the norm within the Indian immigrant population. Nevertheless there are large numbers of Indians, even among the younger and more Americanized second generation, who are apolitical and quite content with the American status quo. Their parents' outlooks, if not wholly accepted, have not been wholly rejected either. For instance a great many younger Indian immigrants are deeply committed to earning money, success, flashy possessions, a well-paid professional job and a house and family in the suburbs—just like their parents. Socially aware Indian-American students sometimes complain that the Indians among their fellow students are mainly interested in "party, party, mix-and-meet." Many younger people also have conventional views of gender relationships.

Second generation female college students, for instance, report that "the guys" among their Indian classmates are friendly, polite and fun to be with but take their male superiority for granted. They consistently ignore women's ideas and opinions, say female students, who complain they are rarely asked to lead Indian student organizations. Much of this social conservatism is bolstered by younger people's strong Indian cultural identity. Proud of being Indian-American, they feel that professional success is their due after their own and their parents' efforts. They also feel that success reflects well on the ethnic group as a whole. Their pride in becoming integrated into American society is mixed with a desire to maintain such aspects of Indian-ness as "real Indian" gender and family roles.

Liberal or radical Indian immigrant activists pose a series of highly uncomfortable challenges to some of these attitudes. Most activists feel both American society and the Indian ethnic group are not perfect; they want to create social change. Activists argue, for instance, that Indians themselves are often the victims of bias, racism and economic exploitation, and urge Indians to come out of a self-imposed ethnic isolation to ally themselves with other social and ethnic groups. They attack homophobia and sexism among Indians; they point out that Indian family structures, plus a group quest for success, sometimes encourage heavy drinking or domestic violence.

This kind of Indian immigrant organizing activity can be viewed as a continuation of a long New York City tradition in which generations of immigrants produced social critique, community organization, labor unions and self-help. Like their nineteenth century European predecessors in New York, some Indian immigrants have seized on American reformist traditions and blended them with the social protest movements and voluntary service organizations of their own Indian pasts. Activists advocate social change through mobilizing the Indian population, but they also advocate breaking through ethnic group boundaries to integrate Indian immigrants into the larger society in new ways. Activist organizations put their clients in touch with city social welfare agencies, health clinics, labor unions, Asian immigrant coalitions, feminist groups, civil rights organizations and networks of liberal non-Indian intellectuals.

Indian immigrant activists' efforts toward social change do not take place without challenge. Most of these groups have been sharply criticized at one time or another by an ethnic elite, and there are often strenuous attempts to prevent them from representing "the Indian community" (see Chapter 3). As one young social worker remarked rather gloomily, "There's still lots of denial out there. Sometimes I think the whole [Indian] community is in denial." Yet a gradual acceptance of these groups has been visible over the years.

THE ENCOUNTER WITH RACISM

For a great many Indians of the second generation, the encounter with American racism comes very early in their schooling, and it places a stamp on their later search for identity. School children encounter racism and stereotyping from non-Indian classmates whose questions and teasing about racial and ethnic identity range from the simply ignorant to the intentionally hostile. A non-Indian school teacher in a well-off New York suburb was extremely distressed about the discussions about racial identity she heard among her first-graders. She said her white students taunted the Indian, Korean and Chinese: "You're not white, you're black!" and "See how dark you are!" Black students also taunted them: "You aren't black like us. You can't even speak English right!" or "You aren't even American." Every year, this teacher said, tearful Asian children approached her to ask, "Teacher, who am I? Am I black? Am I white?" Her attempts to explain that they were neither, but Indian or Korean or Chinese, meant nothing to children so young. A high school student recalled spending her grade school years trying desperately to imitate and be accepted by African-American and Hispanic classmates in the Bronx. She says she even tried for a while to speak with a Puerto Rican accent. This did not save her from mockery or from being asked to do "an Indian rain dance" (Thomas 1995: 23).

Indian students who have such experiences often cannot turn to their parents for guidance, since Indian immigrant adults have rarely experienced this personal racial harassment and can give little advice on countering it. Furthermore many parents, because they are educated, affluent and professional, think of themselves as white and deny that they or their children might be victimized. Alternatively, parents urge their kids to be proud of being Indian, and make valiant efforts to immerse children in Indian culture. Sympathetic teachers offer similar advice, and even try to include bits of Indian culture or history in their curricula, as much to enlighten non-Indian students as to make Indian children feel valued. Yet efforts to provide younger children with an ethnic, rather than a racial, framework for identity, or to have them feel pride in a culture and a country they have never known personally are not always successful in such contexts. Indian-American children still have to contend with popular American prejudices against foreigners. More confusing to them still, they have to contend with American concepts of a world racially polarized into white or black, where few other categories of identity are recognized.

WIDER IDENTITIES, MULTIPLE IDENTITIES

Many Indian-American young people report that it is only when they left home for college that they really begin to understand, and come to terms with, their ethnic and racial identities and the ways these may combine. Not all Indian-American college students are willing to rethink such questions; many graduate with all opinions intact. For the small number who do reexamine their identities, however, the process is often made easier because, away from family surveillance, students can experiment with identity and make individual decisions about how to define themselves. As one recent college graduate explained, "In high school I had no real identity of my own." He traces his own exploration of ethnic and cultural identities to his involvement with a variety of campus organizations. In making the break with the world of their parents, students are sometimes able to draw strength from the experiences of other Asian-American campus and community groups, many of which have been organizing and writing about racism and Asian-American identity since the 1970s (see Omatsu 1994).

Indian-American college students still encounter racial, ethnic or anti-foreign stereotypes among fellow students (see Osajima 1993). Recent graduates, for instance, are bitter about having been mistaken for Middle Easterners during the Gulf War and harassed about being "terrorists." (Indian Hindus seem particularly outraged at being confused with Muslims.) A student who attended a public college in upstate New York explained, "You find yourselves immersed in a redneck town. There are very few people of color around. But the [white] Long Islanders or upstate kids find so many brown people around, they're not used to it."

The relative freedom of college gives Indian-American students a chance to talk about issues of race, ethnicity and identity for the first time with their peers and to develop more complex understandings of both Indian-ness and ethnicity in general. Many students are eager to study aspects of Indian thought or society in academic courses. A few are able to spend time studying or traveling in India and to develop a more sophisticated appreciation of the culture and what it means to call oneself Indian. Most campuses have Indian student associations which sponsor social and cultural events intended to convey a sense of pride in being Indian-American.

More importantly, most college campuses are now ethnically very diverse, so that Indian-American students are for the first time exposed to many varieties of ethnic identity and to different modes of ethnic mobilization. Some Indian student associations have transformed themselves into South Asian student associations, open to Pakistanis, Bangladeshis or Sri Lankans as well as Indians. Such mergers recognize the common cultural elements in these societies but run counter to the advice of Indian parents, who retain deep hostilities towards Muslim Pakistanis and Bangladeshis and insist that Indian culture must be preserved uncontaminated. In spite of promoting a wider sense of identity, many of the Indian and South Asian student associations remain apolitical. An Indian-American student at Columbia in the mid-1980s remembers with dismay how the university's South Asian student association refused to support the national student protests against South African apartheid, even though apartheid discriminated against South African Indians (Sinha 1993: 13).

College campuses may also introduce Indian students to cross-ethnic coalitions. Some Indian students join pan-Asian student associations, working with Korean-Americans and Chinese-Americans for the first time. Indian student groups have also formed coalitions with black and Hispanic groups over particular issues—often issues of racial discrimination. On one New York state university campus a series of e-mail hate messages directed against African-Americans and Asians mobilized the formation of an anti-racist coalition which included black, Hispanic, Korean, Chinese and Indian students.

In encountering older, better-established traditions of ethnic organizing among Asians and African-Americans, young Indian-Americans may be able to think about themselves for the first time as people of color who share common interests with black, Hispanic or other Asian students. Arun, an activist and recent college graduate who headed a campus South Asian student group, recalls being surprised and impressed with the seriousness and militancy of other student ethnic associations. He notes that the wider, cross-ethnic coalitions wielded wider influence on campus than small ethnic organizations with narrow single-culture agendas. He is now involved as the Indian-American representative to a pan-Asian organization in New York.

College campuses expose young Indian-Americans to wide-ranging discussions about class and gender as well as new forms of ethnic organizing. For young people who may have taken their class privileges in U.S. society for granted, who may have only just begun to question traditional gender roles and who never talked seriously about sexuality or sexual orientation, exposure to campus feminists, Marxists and gay activists can be mind-expanding, to say the least. Arun says his college exposure to such variety helped him grow up. "That was the first time I met all different kinds of people, not just my family, or other Indians, or well-to-do white Americans.... I really got a sense of who I am and what I can do." Presented with an array of choices open to them, some young Indian-Americans realize that they can be Asian feminists, leftists of color and gay South Asians and yet simultaneously retain their Indian cultural heritage (see also Radhakrishnan 1994). This represents a qualitative change from the narrow ethnic identity of their parents.

THE "DOTBUSTERS"

Indian immigrants have not, in general, been subject to as many racial attacks as other U.S. minority groups. According to the U.S. Department of Justice, for instance, there were 4755 hate crimes in thirty-two states in 1991. While over thirty-five percent of the crimes were directed against African-Americans, only six percent were directed against Asians (quoted in Gall and Gall 1993: 101). Furthermore most of the victimized Asians were Koreans, Chinese or Vietnamese, not Indians. Nevertheless, Indian immigrants in the U.S. do encounter racism and prejudice. In some areas such as the agricultural valleys of northern California, where Indians have settled in large numbers, youngsters experience daily harassment in school (see Gibson and Bhachu 1991: 69-71). Yet in the New York area Indians have rarely been singled out for prolonged racial harassment.

The one exception was a series of anti-South Asian incidents in New Jersey in 1987, in an area where large numbers of Indians had moved into a decaying industrial town. What are now known as the "dotbuster attacks" in Jersey City, just across the river from New York City, were notable for their severity—one man died and another was maimed for life—and for the apathy with which New Jersey officials responded. Activists look back on those events as a turning point for the New York area Indian immigrant population, which was for the first time forced to deal with external racism and internal class divisions. In a situation of confusion and fear, a group of Indian immigrant students based at Columbia University first took action, not the Indian immigrant leadership. Although no similar incident has erupted since, the questions raised at the time about Indian ethnicity, race, class and ethnic leadership remain relevant.

"Dotbusters" was the name assumed by groups of young white and Hispanic hoodlums in and around Jersey City who began to push, shove and insult Indian housewives who walked down the street wearing saris and bindi (Hindu Indian women's cismetic dot on the forehead). Indian students at a nearby technical college were beaten up by dotbusters. Some Indian and Pakistani stores, homes and cars were vandalized and shopkeepers were threatened. Eventually two young Indian men were set on and brutally beaten. Kaushal Sharan was left with permanent brain damage. Navroze Mody died of injuries inflicted by a group of Hispanic youths. In the midst of these attacks, a New Jersey newspaper received and published an anonymous letter from a group calling itself "the dotbusters," which vowed to drive Indians (or "dotheads") out of the area by violence. Later local high school students began carrying dotbuster "membership cards," mouthing anti-Asian insults and harassing people (see Sethi 1994:244-247). Neither New Jersey police nor public officials were initially willing to acknowledge these attacks as racial bias crimes and prosecution lagged.

The Indian immigrant leadership in the New York area was slow to acknowledge the magnitude of the trouble, its organized nature or its racist basis. Privately many individual Indians confessed to being deeply shaken. One man said, "I didn't think we Indians would ever face this kind of venom here. We're not like that." He went on to add, "I'm scared. I don't know who hates me and who doesn't. Will I be beaten too?" Yet the same man, a resident of a wealthy Westchester suburb, repeated an accusation widely heard among Indians at the time: the largely working-class Jersey City Indians had brought the trouble on themselves by being "too clannish" and by dressing differently from their neighbors. (He conveniently forgot that in other contexts people are honored for retaining their Indian dress and customs.) The Indian immigrant leadership's response to the events pointed to the ways class status affects people's experiences of racism.

At the time of the attacks, many prominent Indians were afraid that if they denounced official apathy as racism, Indians would be equated with hitherto-despised minority groups. Leaders spoke initially of cultural misunderstandings rather than bias attacks. When, after Mody and Sharan were injured, large Indian protest rallies were finally planned, some Indian immigrant leaders were hesitant about accepting offers from African-American leaders to speak at the rallies. Black ministers from New York City recognized bias crime when they saw it and were anxious to form an anti-racist political alliance, but Indian leaders were reluctant to accept public backing from known civil rights activists.

The attacks mobilized a group of 15 Indian-American college students at Barnard College and Columbia University, who called themselves Indian Youth Against Racism (IYAR, which later changed its name to YAAR, or friend). As a member recollected in a 1993 article, "For many of us it was our first active political involvement. IYAR allowed us to dredge up and utilize our own experiences with discrimination, which we had all felt, in some form or another. It was a turning point for all of us, politicizing all of us for the rest of our lives." (Sinha 1993: 14). IYAR members spent weeks talking to the Jersey City Indians, documenting both the attacks and the contours of the Indian immigrant community. "We all had huge worries about authenticity," recalls one young organizer. "We wondered how could we rich [second-generation college] kids go and talk to those people [first generation working-class adults] or organize them? Did we have any right?"

Nevertheless, IYAR activists did organize very successfully over the next several years. The group helped plan rallies, counseled and supported Navroze Mody's distraught parents, and maintained community pressure on New Jersey officials to pursue the cases. Largely as a result of IYAR agitation, Mody's killers were tried as adults in 1989, not as juveniles. Subsequently IYAR lobbied successfully for passage of a bill increasing the penalties for bias attacks in New Jersey. Other group members helped create a training program on bias, cultural diversity and conflict resolution for a local high school where racial and ethnic tension was high. During this process young IYAR activists often felt isolated, even ostracized, by the larger Indian immigrant population. Many fellow students were apathetic and adults were patronizing or even hostile. "It was hard," recalls one woman. "I looked for my community and it wasn't there."

In 1993 Kaushal Sharan had recovered sufficiently from terrible head injuries to press charges against the men who had beaten him in New Jersey in 1987. YAAR members, some of whom were now lawyers, helped win an indictment by getting the federal government to intervene (Sinha 1993: 15-16). To the activists' surprise, a new generation of Indian-American students, largely from the University of Pennsylvania, took a great interest in the Sharan case and attended the trial in large numbers. "A lot of those students were kinda conservative about other things," says a YAAR activist, "like women. They couldn't deal with us women in YAAR....But because of Indian pride and the Indian identity thing, on this case they were right in there with us, every day." Her remarks suggest that, conventional as they are, these students' sense of Indian-American identity is more active and more attuned to racial/ethnic bias than that of their parents.

THE ISSUES OF CLASS

YAAR received help during its years of anti-dotbuster organizing from a pan-Asian group called the Committee Against Anti-Asian Violence (CAAAV). Today several Indian-Americans work with the group, formed in 1986 by young women from other Asian groups. The organization grows from a feminist and leftist Asian-American activist tradition and addresses itself to discrimination, racial crimes and police brutality against all Asians. CAAAV is concerned with economic exploitation of immigrants and is explicit about the role class differences play in marginalizing poorer Asian immigrants in the U.S., both within their own ethnic groups and within the larger society.

Today CAAAV is concerned about possible legislative attempts in New York to replicate California's notorious Proposition 187, which might deny immigrants, even legal immigrants, state social services and benefits. CAAAV is acutely conscious of the ways in which immigrants, particularly Asian immigrants, can be made the scapegoats for New York City's urban ills. The organization is presently focusing on the difficulties of Asian women—particularly Koreans, Thais, Chinese and Bangladeshis—working in New York's thriving, partially illicit sex industry. CAAAV also runs a youth leadership project for Southeast Asians in York, since it identifies Vietnamese and Cambodians as among the poorest and most underserved Asian groups in the New York area.

An organization called the Lease Drivers' Coalition (LDC), is affiliated with CAAAV and serves a large number of South Asian immigrant taxi drivers. LDC was founded in 1992 by South Asian drivers working in conjunction with older, white American drivers who had experience in union organizing. The group addresses the difficulties of the 35,000 New York City taxi drivers, some 90% of them immigrants, who lease their cabs on a daily or weekly basis from taxi owners. Owners now pay over $200,000 for each medallion, which is needed if a yellow cab is to operate legally within the city. Lease drivers, who include large numbers of Indians, Pakistanis and Bangladeshis, rent their cabs from medallion owners for about $1000 a week; they also pay the cost of gas. Usually several drivers share a week's rental and try to make money by driving twelve-hour shifts. Drivers estimate that they earn around $20,000 a year (Rogoff 1995: A17) if they work full-time, that is twelve hours a day for six or seven days a week. LDC recently lobbied the New York City Council, opposing an increase in taxi fares which medallion owners want. LDC argues that the fare increase would drive away passengers and encourage medallion owners to charge lease drivers still higher rents.

South Asian drivers feel victimized by the police as well as medallion owners. Drivers accuse the police of racial and anti-immigrant prejudice and complain that they get little protection from passengers who may rob, beat or even kill them as they work. South Asian drivers were particularly outraged several years ago by police failure to search for a South Asian cab driver whose fellow drivers had reported him missing after his shift. The taxi, with the body of the murdered driver inside, were only located several days later by a fellow cab driver.

At the same time lease drivers accuse the police of harassing them arbitrarily over traffic violations; they add that the police frequently hand out beatings and racial insults to those they stop. LDC is working to organize such drivers and also acting as their advocates with the police, with the city's Taxi and Limousine Commission, and with the city council. LDC hands out leaflets and produces a newsletter in English and two South Asian languages. It provides drivers with legal representation at disciplinary hearings and has organized driver protest rallies over various issues. An LDC organizer remarks that South Asian drivers learn, the hard way, the realities of "being black in New York." At the same time, the organizer says, LDC has to counter the racism of its own members, many of whom are reluctant to pick up African-American passengers and resent regulations requiring them to do so.

CRACKS IN THE INDIAN IMMIGRANT FAMILY

Some of the problems Indian immigrants face have their largest impact within the family. Alcoholism, drug dependency, mental illness, AIDS, domestic violence and divorce do occur in Indian immigrant families, although it is hard to tell how frequent they are. Clearly AIDS affects a very small minority of the Indian immigrant population, while domestic violence is unfortunately more widespread. Such difficulties are intensified because Indians treat these conditions as morally shameful secrets to be hidden; Indians are probably even more reluctant than non-Indians to seek help. Indian immigrants believe instead that families are obliged to endure problems on their own and to conceal them from non-family members. Concerned Indian immigrant social workers and medical personnel have now turned their attentions to breaking down the self-imposed isolation which troubled families create for themselves, as well as to educating the larger Indian population about such problems.

American doctors, psychotherapists and social workers have waged a long battle over the last thirty years to convince Americans that a wide variety of problems are treatable or at least endurable if people can acknowledge them and seek outside support. Things like alcoholism have been redefined as medical conditions rather than as purely moral failures.

Indians trained in medicine, psychiatry and social work are trying to create similar openness and acceptance of therapeutic intervention among Indian immigrants in New York. To do so they must struggle to counteract strong cultural patterns. Substance abuse, mental illness and divorce, not to mention AIDS, carry strong overtones of sinfulness, immorality and divine retribution in the Indian context. People become so paralyzed with shame that they cannot admit that they, or their relatives, drink too much, need anti-depressants, or are separating from a spouse. AIDS, with its implications of homosexuality or drug use, is felt to be so disgraceful that families are tempted to banish or disown those known to be infected.

Indian immigrants' refusal to acknowledge difficulties is amplified by their strong family loyalty. Relatives try to cover up the problems in their midst and to reject outside advice, feeling that "It's nobody else's business." People worry about gossip among other Indians, which tarnishes the whole family, not just to the troubled individual. Women in particular feel obliged by traditions of wifely devotion to support and tolerate their husbands' behavior at all costs. Indians experience an added layer of difficulty in acknowledging problems since, as immigrants, they worry obsessively that the entire group's prestige will be damaged if Indians admit the problems in their midst to non-Indians. They are also anxious to preserve an idealized version of Indian culture and to resist the corrupting influences of American culture. "As though," said a young therapist sarcastically, "nobody back in India ever, **ever** got drunk, had sex or went mad."

Nav Nirman is one of the few organizations in New York which brings cultural understanding to bear in counseling Indian, Pakistani, Bangladeshi and Indo-Caribbean families about drug and alcohol abuse, domestic violence, sexually transmitted disease and intergenerational conflict. The group was started in 1990 by an Indian immigrant businessman. He was first moved to action after several Indian-American college students talked to him about aspects of their own drinking, pot smoking and sex lives which disturbed them. This man realized that local Indians had problems they could not discuss with families and friends, and that they had little contact with New York City's social and educational services. As a first step he himself began counseling people. He also sought further training for himself. Soon afterwards he began a long-drawn-out campaign to convince the Indian immigrant leadership that such services were needed and should be recognized and supported. He also actively sought backing from the office of New York City's mayor.

At first, this man says, other Indians accused him of "fabricating" the distress he reported, and of "spoiling the community's good name" by seeking links to city social service agencies. Some Indian doctors initially felt that they could not intervene since alcoholism or drug use were moral problems, not medical ones.

Gradually Nav Nirman has brought together a group of Indian doctors, social workers and therapists who work with South Asian clients. The organization draws on the energies of young Indians still in training, as well as on those of older, well-established Indian professionals who volunteer their time. In the process the organization has established a reputation with city hospitals and social service agencies, which refer South Asian clients to Nav Nirman. For instance, the group collaborates with the Queens Child Guidance Center, which now, on its own, has established an Asian Outreach Program. Five years after its founding Nav Nirman is a small but influential institution within the New York Indian population. Its organizers feel that its education efforts are gradually changing local Indian attitudes.

An Indian social worker told me about a case which, he believes, illustrates the ways Indian cultural norms affect immigrants' reactions to alcoholism and abuse. The case illustrates the way American-style interventions have an effect, at least in some cases. The man in question began to drink heavily, first to seem sophisticated and "American," later to relieve tension and depression over a faltering career. Eventually he became severely alcoholic and began to beat his wife and children. In keeping with Indian patterns of family loyalty, the woman and the children did their best to conceal the situation and to maintain the man's reputation among other

Indians. When the man lost his job through absenteeism, his wife managed to open a small shop; this, she told friends and relatives, was what her husband had quit his job to do. Actually she ran the store single-handed. In American therapeutic terms, she was an "enabler."

Eventually the man beat his wife so badly that she was hospitalized. The hospital referred her to an Indian social worker. The woman kept an appointment with the social worker only reluctantly, mainly because she was worried about the children's safety. After weeks of counseling with a South Asian therapist, the wife came to understand that her attempts to support her husband were counterproductive, hurting both the children and her husband. She agreed to take her children and move in with relatives. Social workers went with her to court to obtain an order of protection against her husband and helped her get welfare benefits. The social worker believes that the man's enrollment in an alcohol abuse program and his gradual return to sobriety was only made possible when the protective family myth was shattered. Shocked by the loss of his family and his reputation, the man was forced to begin accepting individual responsibility for his drinking and abusiveness.

AIDS and the threat of AIDS are problems which Indian immigrants are just beginning to confront. As among non-Indians, AIDS is surrounded with fear, shame and ignorance. The deep silence within Indian families about sex and sexuality is made more profound by the inhibition younger people feel about discussing such things with older people. As a result the young, the group probably at greatest risk for AIDS, often cannot discuss their sexual orientations, their medical conditions or the complex emotional issues related to sex with their families or even with Indian friends. People who do speak up may find themselves quietly exiled from the family circle at a point in their lives when they most need support.

Two small New York organizations, the South Asian Aids Action (SAAA) and the Asian and Pacific Islander Coalition on HIV/AIDS (APICHA), try to fill some of the gap. These groups offer AIDS prevention information, counseling, support groups for the HIV-positive and for families caring for those sick with AIDS, legal assistance and referrals to social service or medical programs. Both groups do educational work to try to dispel some of the ignorance and myth about homosexuality and AIDS among the larger Indian population. APICHA, which serves a whole range of Asian groups, emphasizes the way language barriers hamper the spread of information and the provision of services, and offers translators to those who need them while visiting clinics or hospitals.

PROBLEMS OF GENDER

Indian immigrant women have particular problems of their own, which have given rise to several Indian women's organizations offering services to Indian and other South Asian immigrant women in the New York area (see Vaid 1989). Most of these groups draw inspiration both from American feminism and from a strong and articulate Indian women's movement.

The need for such organizations is obvious. Indian and other South Asian women are enmeshed in patriarchal family structures. Women born in India, and some of the second generation as well, have absorbed ideals of wifely devotion and self-sacrifice so that they feel guilty if they cannot comply with and submit cheerfully to fathers or husbands. The institutions of arranged marriage and dowry, the fear of divorce, the cultural preoccupations with female chastity and the assumption that men have not only a right but an obligation to control women all make for an explosive mixture in American's cultural context. The situation is still more difficult given the particularly dependent position of first generation immigrant women and the social isolation many experience as immigrants.

One of the largest of the New York area women's organizations is Sakhi for South Asian Women. Founded in 1989, Sakhi (which means woman friend in Hindi) initially focused on helping South Asian women victimized by domestic violence. When notified that a woman was brutalized by her husband, her in-laws or even her own family, Sakhi volunteers would offer support and counseling. If a woman decid-

ed she wanted to leave the household, Sakhi helped women
and children find a place to stay or referred them to battered
women's shelters. Sakhi accompanied women to court to get
orders of protection against husbands or in-laws who threatened to kill them for "dishonoring" the family name by leaving home and discussing their disputes with outsiders. For
abused women it was a tremendous relief to find other South
Asian women who spoke their languages but refused to con-
done traditional South Asian sexist violence.

As Sakhi began to prove itself effective, there was a horri-
fied reaction against it among local Indian immigrants.
Shame and denial were involved, plus an angry defence of
male privilege. Organizers say men whose own female relatives had sought help were particularly virulent, accusing
Sakhi of being a bunch of home-wreckers, lesbian man-hat-
ers, or (simultaneously) of instigating divorces so they could
trap other women's husbands. Gossip labelled women who
worked with the organization, however happily married, the
vengeful victims of domestic violence themselves. Some
younger volunteers say they were branded whores for med-
dling in "unsuitable" issues no young girl should know
about.

Sakhi was also criticized for its extensive links to non-Indian feminist organizations in New York and around the U.S.
The group was accused of bringing "foreign," degenerate
American culture into the heart of the Indian family. Prominent Indian immigrants, women as well as men, felt Sakhi
was exaggerating the extent of domestic violence and ruining
the reputation of the Indian community at large. Others suggested that violence against women was negligible, confined
only to a handful of marginal, poor Indian immigrants: taxi
drivers might beat their wives black and blue and drag them
about by the hair, but software programmers or financial an-
alysts would never do such things. Sakhi and its supporters
have never accepted these interpretations. As one organizer
explained, "Beating and abusing women is part of 'our Indian
culture.' It has a venerable history."

Very quickly Sakhi realized that South Asian immigrant
women's problems were more generalized than abuse.
Women also suffered social isolation, their legal status was

sometimes jeopardized, and many needed employment. The organization began to broaden the kinds of services it offered and the kinds of women it reached out to. For instance, because so many women migrate here as the wives of employed men, their legal right to stay in the U.S. is determined by their husbands' migration status. A woman who comes here from India to join a husband who is a permanent resident has only conditional legal residence here for two years after arrival. If the marriage breaks down in that period, the woman faces the possibility that she will lose her legal immigrant status. Some men even hold the threat over their wives: "Obey me or I'll get you deported." Other women have reported that their husbands kept their "green cards," which identify them as legal permanent residents, to prevent the women from seeking jobs or leaving home.

The circumstances of migration as dependents often isolate women, who have no friends or relatives of their own here to help them in case relations with their husbands degenerate into quarrels, separation, desertion or divorce. Sakhi and other women's organizations repeatedly hear about women who arrive from India to find husbands and sometimes in-laws who are physically or psychologically abusive. Locked into the house, knowing nobody, forbidden to have visitors or to make or receive phone calls, with faltering English and no understanding of their legal rights in the U.S., such women are truly desperate. Some have been rescued because they finally worked up courage to approach somebody outside the family for help. Others have found Sakhi through advertisements that Sakhi broadcasts during Indian immigrant TV programs or flyers passed out at public events.

Poor English, ignorance of American culture and social isolation make it far harder for South Asian immigrant women to support themselves if they leave home. Recently Sakhi has started English literacy classes using trained volunteers. These classes have proved very popular; men beg to join them too. The all-women classes offer not only offer practice in English conversation and reading, but also a forum for discussion in which participants talk about things like how to get around on the New York City subway and read a subway map. Classes also allow women to make new friends. Sakhi has recently launched an effort to organize South Asian domestic workers, trying to offer these exploited and isolated women workers advice about their rights and how to move to better jobs. The group is also preparing a fact sheet for the employers of such workers, outlining the kinds of demands employers can and cannot make on their workers.

Sakhi has responded to criticisms and opposition from fellow immigrants by extending its educational and outreach efforts within the Indian population. These efforts are directed at changing the social norms of the ethnic group, so that the abuse and suppression of women are no longer socially acceptable. At the same time efforts are directed at recruiting members of the second generation and winning funds, approval and volunteer services from young South Asian doctors, lawyers and other professionals. The group uses its expanding corps of volunteers and paid organizers to run workshops, give talks, participate in conferences and talk to non-Indian groups with similar interests. Sakhi often shows its educational video, "A Life Without Fear." By speaking in temples, mosques, churches and in professional, student and community groups, Sakhi is gradually shifting Indian immigrant opinion about women's roles. As the group mobilizes young women of the second generation, who welcome a chance to be of service to fellow Indians, the organization is making feminism a part of their identity. A recent Sakhi fundraiser, at which film maker Mira Nair spoke and showed her new film, was a glittering social event at which many leaders of "the community," as well as young professional men and women, were proud to be seen.

As for those young Indians who discover that they are gay or lesbian, life is not easy. Although New York has a large and well-organized lesbian and gay community, South Asians often feel that these groups do not address cultural issues that concern them, particularly questions of marriage and family. In India homosexual relationships have existed for generations, but virtually everyone pretends not to notice them. This is possible because close same-sex friendships are common and because marriage, children and family are so central to adult identity that few people can imagine life without them. Today a tiny gay and lesbian movement has emerged in some large Indian cities, but it is neither powerful nor visible.

Much of this invisibility carries over into Indian immigrant life, where homosexual love is either ignored or classified as a corrupt American habit. The South Asian Lesbian and Gay Association (SALGA) was founded to provide a place where people can meet, socialize with other South Asians and hold regular discussions and social events. SALGA is also closely connected with other gay and lesbian organizations in New York. In 1995, for the first time, organization members marched in the city's huge Gay Pride Day parade. SALGA's discussion groups for members deal not just with the difficulties people experience in telling their families about their sexual orientation, but also with the intense pressure many—particularly sons—feel to get married and have children. Some people have already succumbed to the pressure to marry before they have been able to define their own attraction to people of the same sex. Others face a double stigma if they take non-Indian lovers.

A young gay man talked about the kind of ostracism he experienced when he finally told his family that he was gay and introduced them to his American lover. They were so distraught, and so visibly ashamed of him, that he finally left New York for the West Coast. His family telephones and sends money and gifts. However, except for one independent-minded sister, they have never visited him or asked him to visit them. To friends and neighbors the parents pretend that the son moved for career reasons and is presently too caught up in his job to get married.

IDENTITY IN OPPOSITION

The various activist organizations which have emerged in recent years are generally small in size, yet they and their ideas are gradually gaining acceptance as part of the mainstream of Indian immigrant life. However the critique these groups offer of accepted attitudes, along with their dedication to social change, still make many Indian immigrants deeply uneasy. The cleavages and discomfort the groups arouse were sharply visible in the summer of 1995, when parade organizers

from the Federation of Indians in America (FIA) denied many
of the activist groups permission to march in the India Day
parade (see Chapter 3). This meant that the activists were not
allowed public symbolic recognition as parts of New York's
Indian community.

The issue of India Day parade participation has been contentious for a long time. For years Sakhi was denied permission to march, but eventually was considered respectable
enough for inclusion. SALGA, the lesbian and gay group,
was officially banned, but in 1994 Sakhi members invited
SALGA members and their banners to join them in the line of
march. Parade organizers were furious, but unable to expel
the interlopers, "under the eyes of the world's cameras," as a
SALGA organizer noted with satisfaction. Not surprisingly,
in 1995 SALGA, Sakhi and other activist groups like LDC/
CAAAV and SAAA were all banned from the parade. Parade
organizers justified their stand by claiming that these "South
Asian" organizations had nothing to do with "the culture and
interests of India" being celebrated by the parade. Various respected Indians who tried to mediate were told privately that
SALGA was a corrupting influence on young Indian-Americans, and that South Asian organizations which included Pakistanis or Muslims were an insult to India on a day
celebrating Indian independence.

The banned groups formed an ad hoc coalition which organized a protest for the event. Arriving early, protesters sta-
tioned themselves across from the reviewing stand where
parade officials and the VIP's of the local Indian population
were gathered. The elite had to spend its time staring at protest signs denouncing intolerance and suggesting "Unity is
Strength." Official speeches were drowned out by cries of
"Shame! Shame! Shame!"

Many Indian immigrants would argue that these internal
quarrels are passing events, embarrassments created by a
handful of unrepresentative trouble-makers, which have no
place in a book about the larger Indian immigrant population. Some will argue that such a discussion disgraces Indian
immigrants. These people and events, however, are important in several respects.

Although the activist groups are small, kept alive by a tiny core of tireless volunteers and paid organizers, the organizations survive because they meet real needs among larger Indian and South Asian immigrant constituencies. By virtue of their energy and perseverance, activists have actually succeeded in changing some people's attitudes and behavior. Furthermore the issues and debates these groups raise—sometimes through confrontational tactics—extend the range of choices and identities Indian immigrants can choose from. In addition to identifying themselves as Indian-American, they now have other, overlapping ethnic, racial, class and gender categories to choose from in defining themselves. Younger people, in particular, sometimes undergo major transformations in outlook and sense of self through contact with activist organizations and participation in political activity. There are now a great many ways of being Indian in the U.S., not all of them compatible with each other. Like the spoonful of yeast added to bread dough, activists become a source of social change within ethnic groups.

Such organizations and such confrontational episodes are also a useful reminder to social scientists that ethnic groups are not monolithic in composition or outlook. Each of the activist organizations discussed here marks real cleavages and real divergences of outlook within the Indian immigrant population. At the same time, each of these activist groups is instrumental in pushing Indian immigrants beyond the limits of the ethnic group and into contacts with non-Indian Americans and American institutions, whether these are alcoholism clinics, feminist law collectives, labor unions or African-American student associations. The processes of immigrant incorporation into American society are more varied than they appear at first. Not all immigrants are drawn directly into America's social and economic mainstream—but they are incorporated nevertheless, into a larger society which is itself highly segmented, contentious and full of contradictions.

Conclusion

Indians are an important part of the large post-1965 Asian migration to the United States; New York and surrounding areas, with a long history of absorbing immigrants, now attract three of every ten Indians arriving to settle in the U.S. As a result, the New York metropolitan area has a wealth of formal and informal Indian immigrant institutions and a rich Indian social life. This book has looked at selected aspects of the area's Indian immigrant world: shopping and consumption, ethnic organizations, public festivals, cultural organizations, religious worship, social and political activism, family life and the relationships between the sexes and between generations.

In describing Indian immigrants' worlds, I have tried to bring out some of the values, both stated and implicit, by which they live. There is an emphasis on education, hard work, self-reliance and family loyalty as well as a strong desire to make money and gain prestige. Pride in being Indian merges into a sense of moral superiority to "the Americans."

Many Indians in the New York area, like Indian immigrants nationally, see themselves as a "model minority" in the U.S., one which has few social problems and is superior to other immigrants and ethnic minorities. This self-image sometimes encourages Indian racism against other ethnic groups; it also makes poor Indian immigrants—a minority within the total population but nevertheless present—invisible to their fellow Indians. Although most Indians settle into a prosperous middle-class professional life within a decade of arrival, a certain number of Indian immigrants never find the dreamed-of professional job and remain members of the American working or lower-middle classes.

What New York City's Indian immigrant leaders speak of as "the Indian community" is not a single community in any functional sense. There are, to be sure, certain shared values and social patterns within the local Indian population, as well as participation in some public ethnic festivals. In general, however, the Indian population is segmented by Indian regional origin and religion, geographically dispersed around a large metropolitan area, and divided by profound class cleavages and different political outlooks. Even family groups are divided by gender and generational outlook.

With so much internal variation and stratification, there are inevitable internal conflicts within the ethnic group as well as conflicts with the larger society. Some of these conflicts have begun to take organizational form in the last ten years as social and political activists, many of them young, address questions like anti-Asian racism, the oppression of women, alcoholism and economic exploitation. In doing so they confront the assumptions and class interests of longer-established Indian immigrant organizations. Conflict and the growth of activism are a useful reminder of how internally diverse immigrant populations can be, and how rapidly their internal configurations shift.

In this book I have tried to place the large Indian migration in the United States in the context of world-wide social and economic changes. Over the last 30 years the restructured economies of the U.S. and other Western countries have created a demand for skilled workers, professionals and large investors. Related economic changes occurring in India over the same period have caused uneven social and economic development, so that a great many young, educated, middle-class Indians now want to migrate abroad to fill those jobs. Today as significant parts of India's urban professional and business classes leave the country, Indians are beginning to talk of the widely scattered Indian immigrant populations as the Indian diaspora. Those in the diaspora who have settled in the U.S. confront the task of inserting themselves into an American middle class via their Indian educational qualifications and class advantages.

The development of a global economy, which moves businesses, jobs and cultural influences back and forth across international borders, has helped create a new kind of migrant, whom I have called transnational. The transnational immigrant has social networks which are not confined by national borders. Indian immigrants in New York may, for instance, maintain important social relationships in India and perhaps in other parts of the Indian diaspora as well. The relative prosperity of Indian immigrants in the U.S. certainly encourages this transnationalism. Prominent among the transnational migrants living in the U.S. are Indian professionals and business people who return periodically to India with money and technical expertise to invest "back home."

Many other Indian immigrants travel back and forth for purely personal reasons, shuttling between India and Indian immigrant communities in the U.S., Britain or Canada. Indian-American New Yorkers typically have transnational kin networks which now stretch across the globe. This extensive international travel and communication is having a cumulative cultural impact on Indian society as well as on the development of a diasporic identity. There is an ongoing debate over the degree to which Indian immigrants living in the U.S. and other parts of the world can still be considered a part of Indian society.

An equally large number of Indian citizens, from grandmothers to religious figures to music promoters, come to the U.S. from India not as immigrants but as regular visitors who travel to keep in touch with relatives, friends, clients, devotees and constituents settled abroad. The travelers' activities, plus Indian and Indian immigrant media, help link the New York Indian immigrant population closely to events in India and other parts of the diaspora. It is striking how quickly anti-Asian racism in Britain or religious conflict in India becomes part of Indian immigrant discourse in New York.

For social scientists, the new complexity of Indian migration and transnational immigrant social life means that research can no longer take place simply within the confines of a single immigrant community. It is imperative to be aware of events, trends and debates going on in India and elsewhere in the diaspora since the various social realms are in constant dialogue. The transnationalism of immigrants also complicates questions of identity, particularly among members of the first generation. In certain contexts Indians may emphasize their identity as members of the world-wide Indian diaspora as well as their ethnicity. Some younger Indian-Americans seem to feel that they have more to learn from South Asian immigrants in Britain than from India itself.

Many of the activities I have described as characteristic of New York's Indian immigrants are closely linked to creation of an ethnic group identity. In daily life food, clothing, music and movies have become cultural markers of Indian-ness. As a result, Indian shopping areas have both straightforward economic functions and an important role in providing goods and services laden with intense symbolic meaning.

Apart from their largely private consumption activities, Indians also take part enthusiastically in urban public festivals organized by Indian immigrant religious, business and ethnic organizations. In addition to heightening Indian immigrants' ethnic consciousness, public festivals dramatize Indians' ethnic group identity before a non-Indian audience of fellow New Yorkers. In general both the public and private efforts to establish and define an Indian-American cultural identity have created an identifiable sense of self among second generation Indian immigrants, who think of themselves as Americans with a prized ethnic cultural heritage.

Some Indian immigrant organizations and leaders have taken on the role of guarding the boundaries of the ethnic group. They attempt to exclude from ethnic events certain organizations they believe discordant with Indian ethnic identity. At present these are groups which call themselves South Asian or pan-Asian, staffed by younger, more liberal Indians and promoting controversial causes such as feminism or gay rights. Many activists believe that it is not the label "South Asian" which makes them insufficiently Indian for inclusion, but rather the gay, lesbian or feminist identities their activism implies. The resulting debate and conflict within the Indian immigrant population suggest the complicated ways in which class, gender and political identities become entwined with ethnic group and racial identities in the U.S.

There are, at the same time, other layers of identity available to Indian immigrants which link them to larger populations. For some, as I mentioned, there is a growing sense of pan-Indian or diasporic identity, developed through travel, investment or devotion to popular music produced in Britain's South Asian communities. A small number of younger people are developing a sense of being "people of color" or Asian-Americans, invoking a shared history of colonialism, marginalization, discrimination and resistance to form alliances with other racial or ethnic minorities.

Members of the immigrant second generation are generally more willing to consider themselves South Asians, on the grounds of cultural similarities to Pakistanis, Sri Lankans or Bangladeshis. Social activists have found that by defining themselves and their groups as South Asian or Asian-American, they can address wider constituencies as well as confront common issues of gender, class, racism or economic exploitation. At present many older Indian immigrants find some of these wider self-identifications threatening and incompatible with Indian-ness. Unlike the young, older Indian immigrants seem more uncomfortable with the recognition of layered, multiple identities, and particularly so when these are invoked in pursuit of non-traditional social activism.

Clearly, the experience of migration and being an immigrant is often confusing, stressful and emotionally wrenching for Indians in this country. Indians, especially those who were born and socialized in India, find themselves in the contradictory position of being generally well-assimilated in economic terms but still culturally distinct. The largest cultural differences between Indian and American patterns of behavior appear to lie in the areas of gender and family life, producing strains between the generations and between men and women. In this case too, a defense of Indian-ness and Indian culture is sometimes invoked to reject social change.

References

Agarwal, Priya
  1991   Passage From India: Post-1965 Indian Immigrants And Their
         Children. Palos Verdes: Yuvati Publications.
Agnihotri, Ajai
  1995   Chicago Man Elected to Bihar Assembly. *News India-Times*
         April 14: 1, 61.
Alba, Richard
  1990   Ethnic Identity: the Transformation of White America. New
         Haven: Yale University Press.
Asian Women United of California (eds.)
  1989   Making Waves, An Anthology of Writings By and About Asian
         American Women. Boston: Beacon Press.
Basch, Linda, Nina Schiller and Cristina Szanton-Blanc
  1994   Nations Unbound, Transnational Projects, Postcolonial Predic-
         aments and Deterritorialized Nation-States. Langhorne,
         Pa.:Gordon and Breach Publishers.
Bhachu, Parminder
  1985   Twice Migrants, East African Sikh Settlers in Britain. London:
         Tavistock Publications.
Bhagwati, Jagdish
  1976   The Brain Drain. International Social Science Journal 28 (4): 692-
         729.
Bogen, Elizabeth
  1987   Immigration in New York. New York: Praeger.
Chawla, Sudershan
  1991   Different By Choice. *In* Asian American Experiences in the
         United States, Oral Histories of First to Fourth Generation
         Americans from China, the Philippines, Japan, India, the Pacific
         Islands, Vietnam and Cambodia. Joann Faung and Jean Lee,
         eds. Jefferson, N.C.: McFarland and Co. Inc.

Cheng, Lucie and Edna Bonacich (eds.)
1984 Labor Migration Under Capitalism: Asian Workers in the United States Before World War II. Berkeley: University of California Press.

Chopra, Sonia
1994 A Whiff of India. *New York Newsday* Aug. 22: A-8.

Clark, Colin, Ceri Peach and Steven Vertovec
1992 South Asians Overseas, Migration and Ethnicity. Cambridge: Cambridge University Press.

Divakaruni, Chitra Banerjee
1995 Arranged Marriage. New York: Anchor Books, Doubleday.

Doyle, Joe and Madhulika Khandelwal
1994 Asian and Pacific Islanders Enumerated in the 1990 Census. Information sheet. Flushing, N.Y.: Asian/American Center, Queens College, CUNY.

Dunn, Ashley
1995 Skilled Asians Leaving U.S. For High-Tech Jobs at Home. *New York Times* February 21: A1, B5.

Espiritu, Yen Le
1992 Asian American Panethnicity, Bridging Institutions and Identities. Philadelphia: Temple University Press.

Fenton, John
1988 Transplanting Religious Traditions, Asian Indians in America. New York: Praeger.

Firestone, David
1995 Major Ethnic Changes Underway. *New York Times* March 29: B1, B4.

Fisher, Maxine
1980 The Indians of New York City. Columbia, Mo.: South Asia Books.

Gall, Susan and Timothy Gall (eds.)
1993 Statistical Record of Asian Americans. Detroit: GaleResearch Inc.

Gardner, Robert W., Bryant Robey and Peter C. Smith
1985 Asian Americans: Growth, Change and Diversity. Population Bulletin 40 (4):1-45.

Gibson, Margaret
1988 Accommodation Without Assimilation, Sikh Immigrants in an American High School. Ithaca: Cornell University Press.

Helweg, Arthur and Usha Helweg
1990 An Immigrant Success Story, East Indians in America. Philadelphia: University of Pennsylvania Press.

Holmes, Steven A.
1995   Congress Plans Stiff New Curb On Immigration, Congress
        Planning to Adopt the Most Stringent Curbs on Immigration in
        71 Years. *New York Times* Sept. 25: A1, A12.

Jennings, James
1994   Conclusion: Racial Hierarchy and Ethnic Conflict in the United
        States. *In* Blacks, Latinos and Asian in Urban America, Status
        and Prospects for Politics and Activism. James Jennings, ed.
        Westport, Conn.: Praeger.

Jensen, Joan
1988   Passage from India, Asian Indian Immigrants in North Ameri-
        ca. New Haven: Yale University Press.

Jha, Alok
1995   Not For God's Sake Alone. *India* Today April 30: 64b-64c.

Khandelwal, Madhulika
        Indian Immigrants in Queens, New York City: Patterns of Spa-
        tial Concentration and Distribution, 1965-1990. *In* Nation and
        Migration: the politics of space in the South Asian diaspora. Pe-
        ter van der Veer, ed. Philadelphia: University of Philadelphia
        Press.

Kwong, Peter
1987   The New Chinatown. New York: Hill and Wang.

La Brack, Bruce
1988   The Sikhs of Northern California 1904-1975. New York: AMS
        Press.

Leonard, Karen
1992   Making Ethnic Choices, California's Punjabi Mexican Ameri-
        cans. Philadelphia: Temple University Press.

Lessinger, Johanna
1993   Business and Success in New York City: Indian Immigrants and
        the American Dream. Paper delivered at conference "The Ex-
        panding Landscape, South Asians in the Diaspora," Columbia
        University March 1993.

———
1992a   Investing Or Going Home? A Transnational Strategy Among
        Indian Immigrants in the United States. *In* Towards a Transna-
        tional Perspective on Migration, Race, Class, Ethnicity and Na-
        tionalism Reconsidered. Nina Schiller, Linda Basch, Cristina
        Blanc-Szanton, eds. New York: New York Academy of Sciences.

———
1992b   Nonresident-Indian Investment and India's Drive for Industrial
        Modernization. *In* Anthropology and the Global Factory, Stud-
        ies of the New Industrialization in the Late Twentieth Century.
        Frances A. Rothstein and Michael L. Blim, eds. New York: Ber-
        gin and Garvey

1990   Asian Indians in New York: Dreams and Despair in the News-
        stand Business. The Portable Lower East Side, special issue on
        Asians in New York. Peter Kwong, ed. 7 (2):73-87.

Lipp, Marty
1994   Reaping the Harvest Music. *New York Newsday* Aug. 15: B5.

Marable, Manning
1994   Building Coalitions among Communities of Color: Beyond Ra-
        cial Identity Politics. *In* Blacks, Latinos and Asians in Urban
        America, Status and Prospects for Politics and Activism. James
        Jennings, ed. Westport, Conn.: Praeger.

Martin, Douglas
1993   Seeking New Ties and Clout, Korean Grocers Join Voices. *New
        York Times* March 22: A1, B6.

Melwani, Lavina
1995   Domestic Workers, Bonded in America. *India Today* Jan. 31:76b-
        76c.

Motwani, Jagat K. and Jyoti Barot-Motwani
1989   Introduction. *In* Global Migration of Indians, Saga of Adven-
        ture, Enterprise, Identity and Integration. Jagat Motwani and
        Jyoti Barot-Motwani, eds. New York: Commemorative volume
        released by The First Global Convention Of People Of Indian
        Origin.

Narayan, Shoba
1995   When Life's Partner Comes Pre-Chosen. *New York Times* May 4:
        C1, C8.

Omatsu, Glenn
1994   The 'Four Prisons' and the Movements of Liberation, Asian
        American Activism from the 1960s to the 1990s. *In* The State of
        Asian America, Activism and Resistance in the 1990s. Karin
        Aguilar-San Juan, ed. Boston: South End Press.

Omi, Michael and Howard Winant
1994   Racial Formation in the United States, From the 1960s to the
        1990s. New York: Routledge.

Radhakrishnan, R.
1994   Is the Ethnic "Authentic" in the Diaspora? *In* TheState of Asian
        America, Activism and Resistance in the 1990s. Karin Aguilar-
        San Juan, ed. Boston: South End Press.

Reimers, David
1992   Still the Golden Door, the Third World Comes to America. New
        York: Columbia University Press.

Roosens, Eugeen E.
1989   Creating Ethnicity, The Process of Ethnogenesis. Frontiers of
        Anthropology Vol. 5. Newbury Park: Sage Publications.

Rustomji-Kerns, Roshni (ed.)
1995   Living In American, Poetry and Fiction by South Asian American Writers. Boulder: Westview Press.

San Juan-Aguilar, Karin
1994   Linking The Issues, From Identity to Activism. In The State of Asian America, Activism and Resistance in the1990s. Karin San Juan-Aguilar, ed. Boston: South End Press.

Saran, Parmatma
1985   The Asian Indian Experience in the United States. New Delhi: Vikas Publishing House Pvt. Ltd.

Saran, Parmatma and Edwin Eames
1980   The New Ethnics, Asian Indians in the United States. New York: Praeger Publishers

Schiller, Nina, Linda Basch and Cristina Blanc-Szanton (eds.)
1992   Towards a Transnational Perspective on Migration, Race, Ethnicity and Nationalism Reconsidered. New York: New York Academy of Sciences.

Sethi, Rita Chaudhry
1994   Smells like Racism, A Plan For Mobilizing Against Anti-Asian Bias. In The State Of Asian America, Activism and Resistance in the 1990s. Karin Aguilar-San Juan, ed. Boston: South End Press.

Shah, Sonia
1994   Presenting The Blue Goddess, Toward a National Pan- Asian Feminist Agenda In The State Of Asian America, Activism and Resistance in the 1990s. Karin Aguilar-San Juan, ed. Boston: South End Press.

Stevenson, Richard
1994   London Journal, Rapping, and No Apologies for a Generation's Rage. New York Times Aug 12: A3.

Takaki, Ronald
1989   Strangers From a Different Shore, a history of Asian Americans. Boston: Little Brown.

Visaria, Pravin and Leela Visaria
1990   India. In Handbook On International Migration. William Serow, Charles Nam, David Sly and Robert Weller, eds. New York: Greenwood Press.

Wei, Willaim
1993   The Asian American Movement. Philadelphia: Temple University Press.

Women of South Asian Descent Collective Staff (eds)
1993   Our Feet Walk The Sky. San Francisco: Aunt Lute Press.

Youssef, Nadia
1992   The Demographics of Immigration, a Socio-Demographic Profile of the Foreign-Born Population in New York State. New York: Center for Migration Studies.

Sethi, Rita Chaudhry
1994   Smells like Racism, A Plan For Mobilizing Against Anti-Asian
        Bias. *In* The State Of Asian America, Activism and Resistance in
        the 1990s. Karin Aguilar-San Juan, ed. Boston: South End Press.

Shah, Sonia
1994   Presenting The Blue Goddess, Toward a National Pan- Asian
        Feminist Agenda *In* The State Of Asian America, Activism and
        Resistance in the 1990s. Karin Aguilar-San Juan, ed. Boston:
        South End Press.

Sinha, Ritu
1993   An Activist Agenda, How young Indian-American political ac-
        tivists are leading the battle against discrimination and racism.